MZ 150 and 250 Owners Workshop Manual

by Stewart W. Wilkins B. Tech.

Models covered:

143 cc:
ES150 Introduced June 1969, discontinued May 1970
ES150/1 Introduced May 1970, discontinued January 1973
ES150/1 Super Introduced April 1973, discontinued Decenber 1976
TS150 Sports Introduced April 1973

243 cc:
ETS250 Trophy Sports Introduced September 1969, discontinued April 1973
ES250/2 Trophy Introduced May 1970, discontinued May 1974
TS250 Introduced April 1973, discontinued December 1976
TS250 Sports Introduced April 1973, discontinued December 1976
TS250/1 Introduced November 1976

ISBN 85696 546 4

© Haynes Publishing Group 1978, 1979

All rights reserved. No part of this book may be reproduced or transmitted in any form or by any means, electronic or mechanical, including photocopying, recording or by any information storage or retrieval system, without permission in writing from the copyright holder.

Printed in England (253 - 6E2)

ABCDE
FGHIJ
KLMNO
PQR

Haynes

**HAYNES PUBLISHING GROUP
SPARKFORD YEOVIL SOMERSET ENGLAND**

distributed in the USA by
**HAYNES PUBLICATIONS INC
861 LAWRENCE DRIVE
NEWBURY PARK
CALIFORNIA 91320
USA**

Acknowledgements

The author wishes to thank Wilf Green Limited the U.K. MZ concessionaires, for supplying the technical information and VEB Motorradwerk, Zschopau, for permission to reproduce some of their illustrations.

Mr. A. Tranter, Principal of Merton Technical College, kindly loaned his ES250/2 model and Jim Patch, of Yeovil Motorcycle Services Limited loaned the TS150 model and supplied all the necessary parts required in the overhauls. The Avon Rubber Company supplied the illustrations and advice about tyre fitting.

Brian Horsfall assisted with the overhauls and also devised methods to overcome the need for service tools. Les Brazier arranged and took the photographs that accompany the text.

I am indebted to Jeff Clew for his patience and editorship in the preparation of this manual and I also wish to express my gratitude to Maggi Loan who typed the original manuscript.

About this manual

The author of this manual has the conviction that the only way in which a meaningful and easy to follow text can be written is first to do the work himself, under conditions similar to those found in the average household. As a result, the hands seen in the photographs are those of the author. Even the machines are not new; examples that have covered a considerable mileage were selected, so that the conditions encountered would be typical of those found by the average owner/rider. Unless specially mentioned and therefore considered essential, MZ service tools have not been used. There is invariably alternative means of loosening or slackening some vital component, when service tools are not available and risk of damage is to be avoided at all costs.

Each of the six Chapters is divided into numbered Sections. Within the Sections are numbered paragraphs. Cross-reference throughout this manual is quite straightforward and logical. When reference is made, 'See Section 6.10' - it means Section 6, paragraph 10 in the same Chapter. If another Chapter were meant it would say 'See Chapter 2, Section 6.10'.

All photographs are captioned with a Section/paragraph number to which they refer, and are always relevant to the Chapter text adjacent.

Figure numbers (usually line illustrations) appear in numerical order, within a given Chapter. 'Fig. 1.1' therefore, refers to the first figure in Chapter 1.

Left-hand and right-hand descriptions of the machines and their components refer to the left and right of a given machine when normally seated facing the front wheel.

Whilst every care is taken to ensure that the information in this manual is correct no liability can be accepted by the author or publishers for loss, damage or injury caused by any errors in or omissions from the information given.

Modifications to the MZ range

Since the introduction of the 150 cc and 250 cc range of MZ motorcycles in 1969, few component changes have been made to the engine although, of course, parts for the two ranges are not interchangeable.

There has, however, been a considerable number of frame and general chassis alterations, Major modifications include the adoption of telescopic front forks, the redesign of several of the headlight units and tanks and, more recently, the introduction of a spine type frame on the TS250 model.

For the purposes of this manual the ES and TS150 models can be considered the same, unless specific mention is made otherwise. This also applies with regard to the ES, ETS and TS250 models, which can be grouped together in similar fashion.

The photographs used in the text are of the TS150 and ES250 models.

Contents

Chapter	Section	Page	Section	Page
Introductory sections	Acknowledgements	2	Introductory to the MZ150 and 250 ranges	5
	About this manual	2	Modifications to the MZ range	2
	Capacities	8	Ordering spare parts	6
	Dimensions and weights	5	Routine maintenance	7
Chapter 1: Engine, clutch and gearbox	Crankshaft assembly	18	Kickstart mechanism	15
	Cylinder barrel	18	Main bearings	19
	Cylinder head	18	Piston and rings	18
	Dismantling the engine/gearbox unit	12, 35	Primary chain	19
			Refitting engine in the frame	28, 50
	Engine/gearbox unit reassembly	19		
Chapter 2: Fuel system and lubrication	Air cleaner	58	Petrol/oil mix correct ratio	53
	Carburettor	56	Petrol tank	53
	Engine/gearbox lubrication	59	Petrol tap	54
	Exhaust system - cleaning	59		
Chapter 3: Ignition system	Automatic ignition advance unit	61	Ignition coil	61
	Condenser	61	Spark plugs	65
	Contact breaker	62	Timing - ignition	65
Chapter 4: Frame and forks	Centre stand	73	Suspension units	72
	Footrests	73	Speedometer and cable	73
	Frame - examination	73	Steering head bearings	71
	Front forks - Earles type	70	Swinging arm	72
	Front forks - Telescopic	70		
Chapter 5: Wheels, brakes and tyres	Bearings - front	77	Final drive chain	84
	- rear	79	Sprocket - rear wheel	84
	Brake adjustment - front	81	Tyres	84
	- rear	81	Wheels - front	76
	Cush drive	81	- rear	79
Chapter 6: Electrical equipment	Battery	88	Headlamp	89
	Charging light	91	Horn	89
	Direction indicators	89	Ignition and light switch	88
	Dynamo	92	Rear and stop lamp	89
	Fuse location	88	Regualtor	91
Chapter 7: TS250/1 Model	Bulb removal	113	Five speed gearbox	103
	Engine removal	103	Kickstart	108
	Front forks	108 - 109		

NB. Specifications and general description are given at the beginning of each Chapter.
   Fault diagnosis is given at the end of each Chapter

Wiring diagrams   94 - 98, 115
Metric conversion tables   116, 117
Index   118, 119

1975 MZ 250 cc TS250 model

1971 MZ 250 cc ES250/2 model

Introduction to the MZ 150 and 250 ranges

The ES150 model was first imported into this country in June 1969; this was followed by the ETS150 Trophy model in September of the same year. The Trophy version was a similar machine but had a slightly more powerful engine, telescopic front forks and a restyled tank and headlight.

Engine power was upped again in May 1970 when the ES150/1 model was introduced. This was the immediate forerunner of the current ES150/1 Super and its sports version, the TS150 Sports, both of which were first seen in the UK during April 1973.

The 250 cc range commenced about the same time, during September 1969, with the telescopic-forked ETS 250 Trophy Sports, using a completely different, rubber mounted engine unit. First additions to the 250 cc range were the ES 250/2 Trophy and Trophy de luxe models which, although fitted with the same engine and similar frame, were vastly different in appearance with their Earles-type front forks and slimline, unit-styled tank and headlamp.

The ETS model was dropped during April 1974, at the same time as the current TS250 and TS250 Sports models were introduced. TS models are very similar in appearance, taking their styling from the earlier ETS models and are now the only 250's available, the ES250's having been discontinued in 1974.

Dimensions and weights

	ES150	TS150	ES250	TS250
Wheelbase - mm	1270 (50.8 in.)	1305 (52.2 in.)	1325 (53 in.)	1380 (55.2 in.)
Length - mm	1990 (79.6 in.)	2050 (82 in.)	2090 (83.6 in.)	2200 (88 in.)
Width (with mirror) - mm	750 (30 in.)	730 (29.2 in.)	862 (34.5 in.)	750 (30 in.)
Height - mm	1150 (46 in.)	—	1060 (42.4 in.)	—
Ground clearance (loaded) - mm	100 (4 in.)	140 (5.6 in.)	170 (6.8 in.)	160 (6.4 in.)
Weight - kg	112 (246.4 lbs)	103.5 (227.7 lbs)	155 (341 lbs)	151 (332 lbs)
Carrying capacity - kg	158 (348 lbs)	—	165 (363 lbs)	169 (372 lbs)

Ordering spare parts

When ordering spare parts it is advisable to deal direct with an official MZ agent, who should be able to supply most of the parts ex-stock.

Always quote the engine and frame numbers in full. The frame and engine number of the 150 model is located on the front engine mounting and front of the crankcase respectively. On models with the Earles type forks the frame number is on the fork carrier, while on models fitted with telescopic front forks the frame number is stamped on the steering head column.

The engine number of all 250 models is located on the rear right-hand side of the crankcase, above the gearbox sprocket.

It is advisable to include a note of the colour scheme, especially if any cycle parts are to be included in the order. Use only genuine MZ parts. A few pattern parts are available, sometimes at cheaper prices but there is no guarantee that they will give such good service as the originals they replace. Retain any worn or broken parts until the replacements have been obtained; they are sometimes needed as a pattern to help identify the correct replacement when design changes have been made during a production run.

Some of the more expendable parts such as spark plugs, bulbs, tyres, oils and greases etc can be obtained from accessory shops and motor factors, who have convenient opening hours, charge lower prices and can often be found not far from home. It is also possible to obtain parts on a mail order basis from a number of specialists who advertise regularly in the motorcycle magazines.

Frame number (Earles fork models)

Frame number (alternative location)

Engine number

Routine maintenance

Periodic routine maintenance is a continuous process that commences immediately the machine is used and continues until the machine is no longer fit for use. It must be carried out at specific mileage recordings, or on a calendar basis if the machine is not used regularly, whichever is the soonest. Maintenance should be regarded as an insurance policy, to help keep the machine in the peak of condition and to ensure long, trouble-free use. It has the additional benefit of giving early warning of any faults that may develop and will act as a safety check, to the obvious advantage of both rider and machine alike.

The various maintenance tasks are described, under their respective mileage and calendar headings. Accompanying diagrams are provided, where necessary. It should be remembered that the interval between the various maintenance tasks serves only as a guide. As the machine gets older, is driven hard or is used under particularly adverse conditions, it is advisable to reduce the interval between each check.

If a specific item is mentioned but not described in detail, it will be covered fully in the appropriate Chapter. No special tools are required for the normal routine maintenance tasks. Those contained in the tool kit supplied with every new machine will suffice, but if they are not available, the tools found in the average household will make an adequate substitute.

Fortnightly or every 600 miles

Lubricate clutch worm
Check oil level in gearbox
Check brakes
Oil rear chain

3 monthly or every 1500 miles

Tap dust from air filter
Check tightness of engine bolts
Check spark plug gap
Check contact breaker setting and oil felt pad
Check battery electrolyte level
Adjust chain tension
Grease front swinging arm (where applicable)
Grease rear swinging arm

6 monthly or every 3000 miles

Check carburettor
Check petrol tap
Examine cables and fuses
Adjust steering head bearing

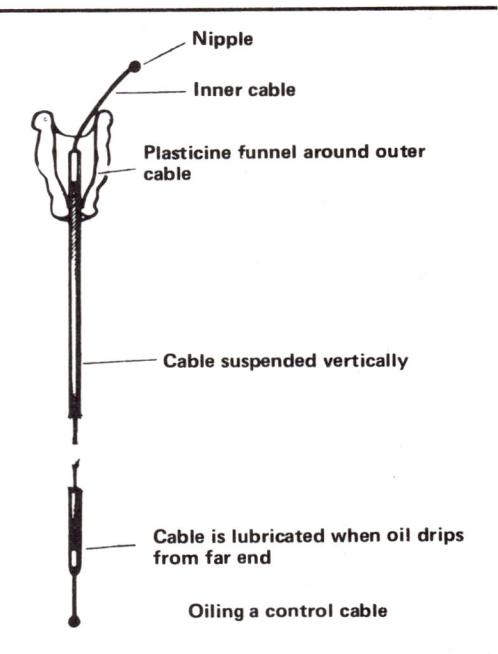

Oiling a control cable
(Nipple, Inner cable, Plasticine funnel around outer cable, Cable suspended vertically, Cable is lubricated when oil drips from far end)

Grease speedometer drive
Lubricate handlebar levers
Lubricate control cables and twistgrip
Grease speedometer cable

Yearly or every 6000 miles

Renew spark plug
Check dynamo
Repack steering head bearings with grease
Repack wheel bearings with grease
Remove and check rear chain

Yearly or every 9000 miles

Renew air filter
Change gearbox oil

Note: No specific mention has been made of the tyre wear since it is assumed the rider will maintain a regular check. Apart from the statutory requirement relating to the minimum depth of tread permissible, a tyre that has cracked or damaged sidewalls should also be replaced immediately, in the interests of safety.

Quick glance maintenance data

	ES150, TS150	ES250, TS250
Engine capacity - cc	150	250
Spark plug gap - mm	0.5 (0.020 in.)	0.5 (0.020 in.)
Contact breaker gap - mm	0.4 (0.016 in.)	0.3 (0.012 in.)
Tyre pressure - p.s.i.		
Front	22	22
Rear solo	28	28
Rear pillion	31	31
Gearbox oil capacity - cc	450	750
Petrol: oil ratio		
TS250 model	50 : 1	
All other models	33 : 1	
Fuel tank (total) - litres	12 (12.5)*	16 (12.5 or 17.5)*+
Imp. gallons	2.5 (2.75)* approx.	2.5 (2.75 or 3.85)*+
Fuel tank reserve - litres	1.5	1.5
Imp. pints	2.5 approx.	2.5 approx.
Suspension		
Front - (cc)	80 (220)*	80 (215)*
Rear - (cc)	80 (70)*	70

*Figures in brackets refer to TS models where different from ES models

+The ETS model is fitted with a 22 litre (4.75 Imp. gallon) capacity tank

Recommended lubricants

Engine	Castrol TT two-stroke oil
Gearbox	Castrol ST (90)
Grease nipples	Castrol LM Grease
Control cables	Castrol Everyman Oil
Telescopic forks	Castrol Shockol or Fork Oil
Final drive chain	Castrol Chain Lubricant

Chapter 1 Engine, clutch and gearbox

Contents

150 cc models

General description	1
Operations with engine in frame	2
Removing the engine/gearbox unit	3
Dismantling the engine/gearbox unit - general	4
Preventing the engine from turning both for dismantling and reassembly purposes	5
Dismantling the engine/gearbox unit - removing the cylinder head, barrel and piston	6
Dismantling the engine/gearbox unit - removing the dynamo and neutral light switch	7
Dismantling the engine/gearbox unit - removing the gearbox sprocket and exhaust mounting brackets	8
Dismantling the engine/gearbox unit - removing the right-hand external oil seals	9
Dismantling the engine/gearbox unit - removing the left-hand engine cover	10
Dismantling the engine/gearbox unit - removing the clutch, primary drive and kickstart mechanism	11
Dismantling the engine/gearbox unit - separating the crankcase	12
Dismantling the engine/gearbox unit - removing the crankshaft and gearbox components	13
Cylinder head - examination and renovation	14
Cylinder barrel - examination and renovation	15
Piston and piston rings - examination and renovation	16
Small end bearing - examination and renovation	17
Crankshaft assembly - examination and renovation	18
Main bearings and oil seals - examination	19
Crankcases - examination and renovation	20
Primary chain - examination and renewal	21
Clutch assembly - examination and renovation	22
Gearbox components - examination and renovation	23
Reassembling the engine/gearbox unit - general	24
Reassembling the engine/gearbox unit - fitting bearings and oil seals into crankcase	25
Reassembling the engine/gearbox unit - replacing the gears and selector	26
Reassembling the engine/gearbox unit - adjusting and setting the gear selector mechanism	27
Reassembling the engine/gearbox unit - replacing the crankshaft and joining the crankcase	28
Reassembling the engine/gearbox unit - replacing the right-hand external oil seals	29
Reassembling the engine/gearbox unit - replacing the kickstart mechanism	30
Reassembling the engine/gearbox unit - replacing the primary drive and clutch	31
Reassembling the engine/gearbox unit - replacing the left-hand engine cover	32
Reassembling the engine/gearbox unit - replacing the gearbox final drive sprocket	33
Reassembling the engine/gearbox unit - replacing the dynamo, neutral light switch and exhaust mounting brackets	34
Reassembling the engine/gearbox unit - replacing the piston, cylinder barrel and head	35
Reassembling the engine/gearbox unit - refitting the engine in the frame, adjustment of neutral light switch and clutch	36
Starting and running the rebuilt engine	37
Fault diagnosis - engine	38
Fault diagnosis - gearbox	39
Fault diagnosis - clutch	40

250 cc models

General description	41
Operations with engine in the frame	42
Removing the engine/gearbox unit	43
Dismantling the engine/gearbox unit - general	44
Preventing the engine from turning for dismantling and reassembly purposes	45
Dismantling the engine/gearbox unit - removing the cylinder head, barrel and piston	46
Dismantling the engine/gearbox unit - removing the gearbox sprocket and engine mounting strap	47
Dismantling the engine/gearbox unit - removing the dynamo	48
Dismantling the engine/gearbox unit - removing the left-hand engine cover	49
Dismantling the engine/gearbox unit - removing the kickstart mechanism	50
Dismantling the engine/gearbox unit - removing the clutch and primary drive	51
Dismantling the engine/gearbox unit - removing the oil seal cups	52
Dismantling the engine/gearbox unit - separating the crankcase	53
Dismantling the engine/gearbox unit - removing the crankshaft and gearbox components	54
Cylinder head - examination and renovation	55
Cylinder barrel - examination and renovation	56
Piston and piston rings - examination and renovation	57
Small-end bearing - examination and renewal	58
Crankshaft assembly - examination and renovation	59
Main bearing and oil seals - examination	60
Crankcase - examination and renovation	61
Clutch assembly - examination and renovation	62
Gearbox components - examination and renovation	63
Engine mountings - examination and renewal	64
Reassembling the engine/gearbox unit - general	65
Reassembling the engine/gearbox unit - fitting bearings and oil seals into crankcase	66
Reassembling the engine/gearbox unit - replacing the gears and selector drum	67
Reassembling the engine/gearbox unit - replacing the gear selector mechanism	68
Reassembling the engine/gearbox unit - replacing the crankshaft and joining the crankcase	69
Reassembling the engine/gearbox unit - reassembling the clutch	70
Reassembling the engine/gearbox unit - replacing the primary drive and clutch	71
Reassembling the engine/gearbox unit - replacing the kickstart, left-hand engine cover and clutch operating mechanism	72
Reassembling the engine/gearbox unit - replacing and shimming the oil seal cups	73
Reassembling the engine/gearbox unit - replacing the dynamo	74
Reassembling the engine/gearbox unit - replacing the gearbox sprocket	75
Reassembling the engine/gearbox unit - replacing the piston, cylinder barrel and head	76
Reassembling the engine/gearbox unit - refitting the engine in the frame	77
Starting and running the rebuilt engine	78
Fault diagnosis - engine	79
Fault diagnosis - gearbox	80
Fault diagnosis - clutch	81

Chapter 1: Engine, clutch and gearbox

Specifications

Engine				
	Air cooled single cylinder two-stroke			
Model(s)	ES150	TS150	ES250	TS250
Stroke - mm	58	58	65	65
Bore - mm	56	56	69	69
Swept volume - cc	143	143	243	243
Compression ratio	9 : 1	—	8.5	9.5 - 10 : 1
Output hp @ rpm	10 @ 5500 - 5800	12.5 @ 6000 - 6300	17.5 @ 5000 - 5300	21 @ 5000 - 5500
Torque - kg/m @ rpm	1.35 (max.)	1.45 @ 5000 - 5500	2.5 @ 4500 - 4700	2.7 @ 4700 - 5000
Port timing (crank angle)				
Inlet (port with point)	142.5	150	140	155
Inlet (port without point)	126	—	—	—
Transfer	110	115	113	118
Exhaust	150	165	160	170

Gearbox

Model(s)	ES150, TS150	ES250, TS250
Gear ratios		
First	3.05 : 1	2.77 : 1
Second	1.805 : 1	1.8 : 1 (1.63 : 1 on some ES250 models)
Third	1.285 : 1	1.23 : 1
Fourth	1 : 1	0.92 : 1
Primary drive ratio : 1	2.31	2.43
Bearing numbers		
Layshaft (input)		6204
Mainshaft (output)		6203 / 6203 / 6204
Clutch shaft	6202	
Counter shaft	6201	
Shaft wheel	6004	

Assembly dimensions and wear limits
(all dimensions in mm)

Model(s)	ES150, TS150	ES250	TS250
Clutch plate thickness			
New	3.4 ± 0.1 (0.134 in. ± 0.004 in.)	3.0 ± 0.1 (0.118 in. ± 0.004 in.)	3.0 ± 0.1 (0.118 in. ± 0.004 in.)
Clutch plate - wear limit	− 0.2 (0.008 in.)	− 0.3 (0.008 in.)	− 0.3 (0.008 in.)
Pressure spring length	49 (1.93 in.)	28.3 ± 0.6 (1.113 in. ± 0.024 in.)	28.3 ± 0.6 (1.113 in. ± 0.024 in.)
Crankshaft max. out of true	0.02 (0.0008 in.)	0.03 (0.0012 in.)	0.02 (0.0008 in.)
Big-end radial play New	0.015 - 0.030 (0.0006 - 0.0018 in.)	0.015 - 0.030 (0.0006 - 0.0018 in.)	0.015 - 0.030 (0.0006 - 0.0018 in.)
Big-end radial play Wear limit	0.05 (0.002 in.)	0.05 (0.002 in.)	0.05 (0.002 in.)
Small-end clearance	0.020 - 0.030 (0.0008 - 0.0012 in.)	0.020 - 0.030 (0.0008 - 0.0012 in.)	0.020 - 0.030 (0.0008 - 0.0012 in.)
Small-end wear limit	0.045 (0.0016 in.)	0.045 (0.0016 in.)	0.045 (0.0016 in.)
Piston/barrel assembly clearance	0.04 (0.0016 in.)	0.04 (0.0016 in.)	0.04 (0.0016 in.)
Piston/barrel wear limit	0.1 (0.004 in.)	0.1 (0.004 in.)	0.1 (0.004 in.)
Piston oversizes	8 x 0.25 (0.010 in.)	8 x 0.25 (0.010 in.)	8 x 0.25 (0.010 in.)
Piston - max. oversize	+ 2 (0.080 in.)	+ 2 (0.080 in.)	+ 2 (0.080 in.) (0.082 + 0.0008 in.)
	ES150, TS150	ES250	TS250
Piston ring groove width	2 + 0.05 (0.080 in. + 0.002 in.)	2 + 0.05 (0.080 in. + 0.002 in.)	2.06 + 0.02 Top 2.04 + 0.02 2nd & 3rd (0.081 + 0.0008 in.)

Chapter 1: Engine, clutch and gearbox 11

Piston ring groove wear limit	2.10 (0.084 in.)	2.10 (0.084 in.)	2.10 (0.084 in.)
Piston ring gap	0.2 (0.008 in.)	0.2 (0.008 in.)	0.2 (0.008 in.)
Piston ring gap wear limit	1.5 (0.060 in.)	1.6 (0.063 in.)	1.6 (0.063 in.)

For axial clearances on the 250 models see illustration.

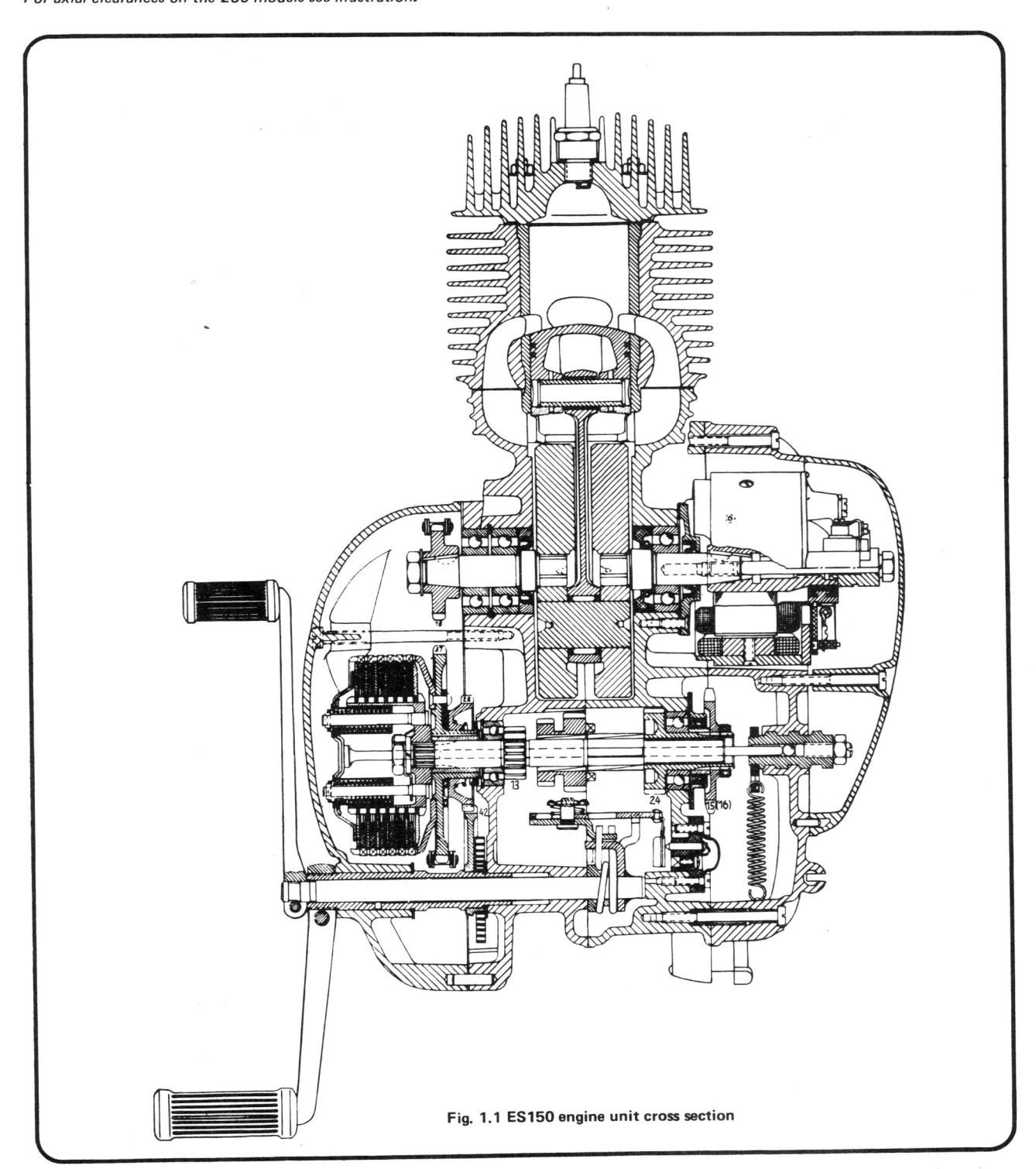

Fig. 1.1 ES150 engine unit cross section

Chapter 1: Engine, clutch and gearbox

150 cc models

1 General description

The ES and TS150 models use basically the same engine, the difference in output being obtained by altering the timing and shape of the ports. The engines are air-cooled, single cylinder two-strokes, utilising a loop scavenging system. Lubrication for the engine is provided by a petroil mixture. The gearbox and clutch have their own integral oil supply.

The crankshaft runs in three ball journal bearings, two on the primary drive side and one on the dynamo side. The connecting rod is fitted with a roller big end and a phosphor bronze small end.

The clutch is mounted on the gearbox mainshaft and is driven by chain from the crankshaft sprocket. A four speed gearbox is fitted to all models.

The electrical system is 6 volt. The dynamo armature is directly mounted on the right-hand end of the crankshaft.

2 Operations with the engine in the frame

It is not necessary to remove the engine unit from the frame unless renewal of, or access to, the following components is required.
1 Main bearings
2 Crankshaft assembly
3 Gear cluster, selector or bearings

3 Removing the engine/gearbox unit

1 Remove the left-hand cover and disconnect the wires from the battery.
2 Remove the exhaust pipe to barrel ring nut using a C-spanner. Unscrew the bolt where the exhaust pipe joins the silencer. Remove the bolt from the rear silencer stay. The exhaust system is now free to be lifted clear.
3 Pull the rear brake cable from the lug in the right-hand engine cover.
4 Either remove the carburettor completely, or remove the throttle slide by undoing both the top ring nut and the cold start device. Hang both safely out of the way. If removing the carburettor manifold complete, note the arrangement of the carburettor insulator and gaskets.
5 Slacken both the gear lever and kickstart lever pinch bolts and pull the levers off their splined shafts.
6 Remove the screw in the right-hand outer engine cover and lift off the cover.
7 Disconnect the wires from the dynamo, noting their positions. Remove the spark plug cap.
8 Unscrew the two screws in the right-hand engine cover and lift off the cover. Unhook the clutch cable.
9 Disconnect the rear chain at its spring link.
10 Disconnect the neutral light switch lead.
11 Remove the rubber plugs concealing the two rear engine mounting bolts. Remove the bolts, using a socket or box spanner.
12 Remove the front engine mounting bolt. The engine should now be free to be lifted upwards and out from the right-hand side of the frame. Before removing the engine, check that all the necessary cables and wiring have been disconnected.

4 Dismantling the engine/gearbox unit - general

1 Before undertaking any work on the engine it should be thoroughly cleaned with a proprietary degreaser to prevent the ingress of dirt and grit particles into the engine.
2 Some of the screws in the engine are very tight and it is

3.2 Remove the exhaust pipe nut and ...

3.2a ... centre clip bolt and ...

3.2b ... rear stay bolt

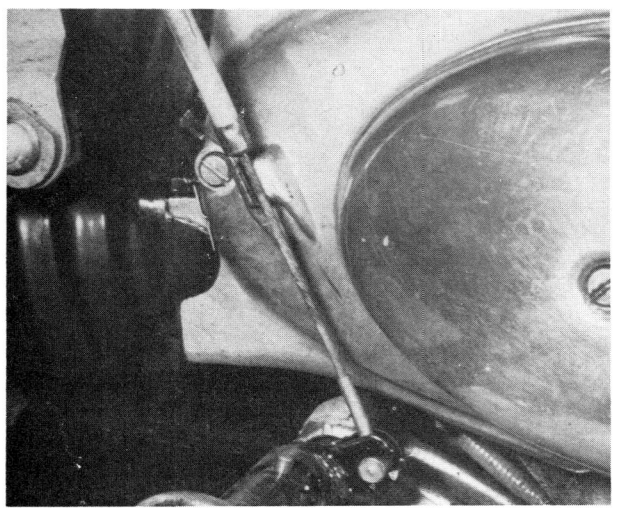

3.3 Unhook the rear brake cable

3.4 Unscrew the cold start plunger and ...

3.4a ... carburettor top

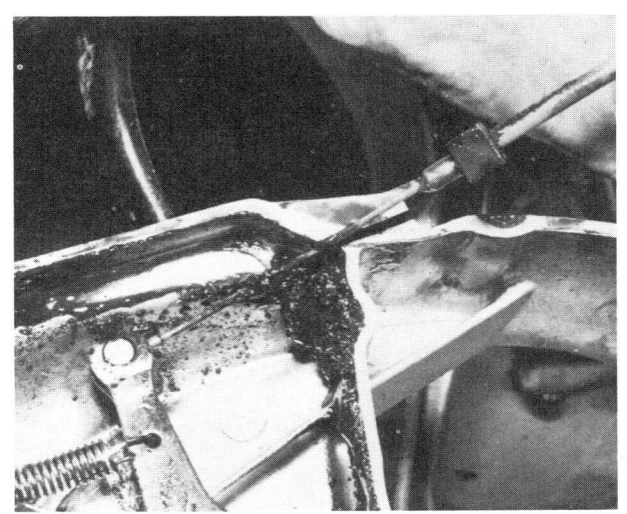

3.8 Unhook the clutch cable

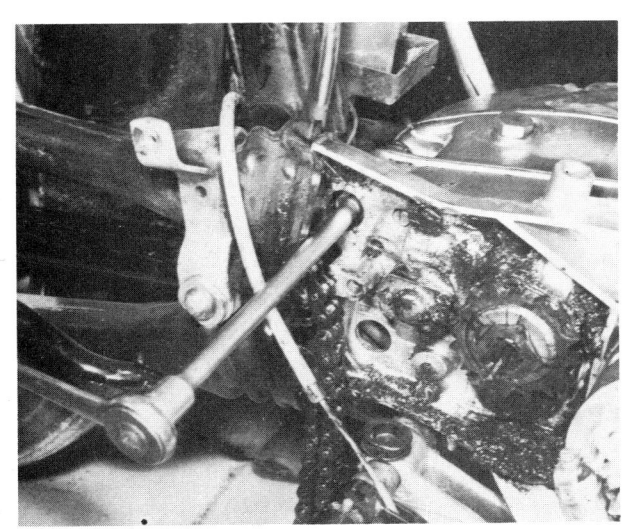

3.11 Remove the top and ...

3.11a ... bottom rear engine mounting bolts

Chapter 1: Engine, clutch and gearbox

strongly advisable to have an impact screwdriver available.

3 Do not use force to remove any part unless specific mention is made in the text. If any component is difficult to remove, first check that everything has been dismantled and/or loosened in the correct sequence.

4 All threads are right-hand unless specific mention is made in the text.

5 Preventing the engine from turning both for dismantling and reassembly purposes

1 It is often necessary to stop the engine from rotating so that a component can be removed or tightened eg; engine sprocket nut, or clutch centre nut. One way of achieving this that can be used both during dismantling and reassembly, is by placing a round metal bar through the small end boss and resting this bar on two pieces of wood placed on top of the crankcase mouth. On no account must the metal bar be allowed to bear directly down onto the gasket face of the crankcase mouth otherwise damage will occur and cause a loss of primary compression.

2 This method can, of course, be used only when the cylinder head, cylinder barrel and piston, have been removed.

6 Dismantling the engine/gearbox unit - removing the cylinder head, barrel and piston

1 Remove the four cylinder head nuts in a diagonal sequence to avoid distorting the head. Lift the head off the studs.

2 Slide the barrel off the studs whilst supporting the piston to prevent it or the rings from damage. If the barrel is tight, slacken off the two screws, one front, one rear, in the top of the crankcase mouth.

3 It is advisable to stuff the open crankcase mouth with clean rag to stop anything falling in and also to prevent damage by the connecting rod hitting the crankcase.

4 Remove the circlips from the piston and press out the gudgeon pin. If the pin is a tight fit, gently heat the piston; a rag soaked in boiling water should suffice.

7 Dismantling the engine/gearbox unit - removing the dynamo and neutral light switch

1 Undo the two screws that retain the dynamo outer and lift the unit out. Be careful not to damage the resistor coil when handling the unit.

2 Lock the engine as described in Section 5.

3 Undo the dynamo armature bolt. Remove the contact breaker cam. The armature is held in position by a Woodruff key in a tapered shaft. If an extractor is not available, use the front crankcase clamp bolt in conjunction with a short spacer (a length of 6 mm bolt), as an extractor. Screw this into the armature until pressure is felt, then hit the end of the bolt smartly, to release the armature from the tapered shaft.

4 Remove the Woodruff key from the tapered shaft.

5 Undo the two screws retaining the neutral light switch and pull the switch out of the crankcase.

8 Dismantling the engine/gearbox unit - removing the gearbox sprocket and exhaust mounting brackets

1 Pull out the clutch operating push rod.

2 Knock back the tab on the locking washer and undo the gearbox sprocket. It has a **left-hand** thread. Lock the engine by putting it in gear and holding it as described in Section 5.

3 Lift off the sprocket and lock washer from the splined shaft.

4 Remove the exhaust mounting straps by undoing the two retaining bolts.

6.2 Slide the barrel off whilst supporting the piston

6.4 Remove the circlips and ...

6.4a ... push out the gudgeon pin

Chapter 1: Engine, clutch and gearbox

7.3 Remove the armature bolt and lift off the cam

7.3a Extract the armature by using a spacer and bolt

9.1 Remove the crankshaft oil seal cup. Note the shims

9.2 Remove the gearbox oil seal cup and spacing collar and shims where fitted

9 Dismantling the engine/gearbox unit - removing the right-hand external oil seals

1 Remove the four screws in the crankshaft oil seal cup and lift the cup off.
2 Remove the five screws in the gearbox oil seal cup and lift off the cup.

10 Dismantling the engine/gearbox unit - removing the left-hand engine cover

1 Remove the four screws retaining the left-hand cover (the 5th is an oil level screw) and lift it off. The cover is located in position by dowels and may require the careful use of a soft faced hammer to loosen it. Do not use a screwdriver.

11 Dismantling the engine/gearbox unit - removing the clutch, primary drive and kickstart mechanism

1 To remove the clutch pressure plate it is necessary to compress the springs and remove the pins. This can be accomplished by pressing down the locating collars with an open-ended spanner and pulling out the pin with a pair of pliers. It may be necessary however, to make up a tie strip to go between the two long right-hand cover screws. This can then be used as a fulcrum point to compress the springs by levering with an open-ended spanner.
2 After removing the six pins, lift out the locating collars, springs and cups, followed by the clutch pressure plate, clutch plates and mushroom.
3 Knock back the tab on the clutch centre lock washer. Prevent the engine from turning and remove the nut. This has a **left-hand** thread. Lift out the clutch centre.
4 Slacken the engine sprocket nut (do not remove as it will prevent the thread being damaged when using the puller) and pull the sprocket off the tapered shaft, using a universal extractor. Remove the engine sprocket nut and washer.
5 Remove the thrust washer from the kickstart shaft.
6 Lift off the clutch drum, chain and engine sprocket as a unit. Note the thrust washer behind the clutch drum plain bearing bush.
7 Remove the Woodruff key from the crankshaft.
8 The kickstart ratchet is located behind the clutch drum. To dismantle, remove the wire circlip which allows the spring cup washer, spring and ratchet gear to be removed from the drum.
9 Lift out the kickstart shaft and quadrant. Take care since the clock type spring is under tension. Note the thrust washer fitted behind the spring.

11.1 Method of compressing the clutch springs

11.2 Lift out the clutch springs and ...

11.2a ... plates and ...

11.2b ... mushroom

11.3 Knock down the tab of the lockwasher and ...

11.3a ... lift out the clutch centre

Chapter 1: Engine, clutch and gearbox

11.4 Use puller for sprocket. Note use of nut to protect thread

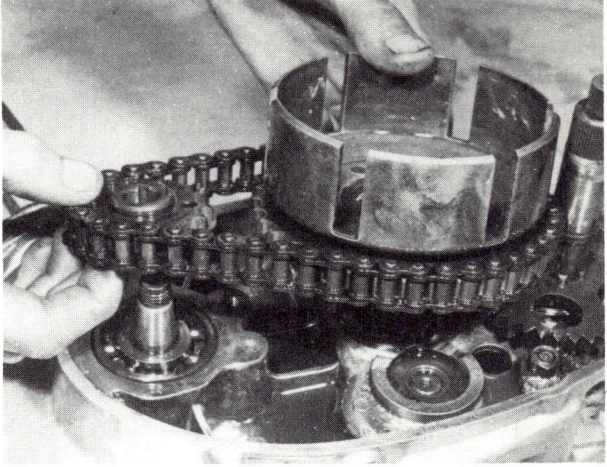

11.6 Lift off the primary drive as a unit

11.8 Remove wire circlip to dismantle kickstart ratchet

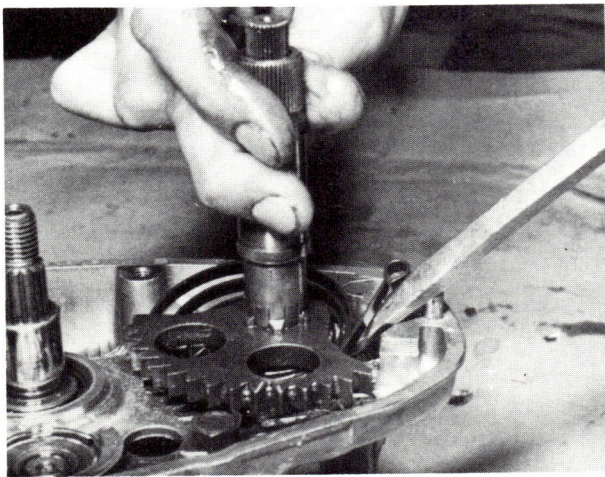

11.9 Unhook the kickstart return spring

12 Dismantling the engine/gearbox unit - separating the crankcase

1 Drive out the two hollow dowels at the front and rear mounting bolt holes.
2 Remove the fourteen crankcase screws.
3 The crankcase is now ready to be parted. It will probably be very difficult to separate, but a soft faced hammer can be used cautiously, if necessary. When parted, the gearbox and crankshaft should remain in the left-hand crankcase. Do not use a screwdriver to separate the halves, since it will damage the jointing surfaces.

13 Dismantling the engine/gearbox unit - removing the crankshaft and gearbox components

1 Remove the crankshaft from the left-hand crankcase.
2 Knock back the tab on the lock washer and undo the nut of the selector fork pin which is located in the clutch side of the crankcase half. Unscrew the selector fork pin.
3 Knock back the tab on the lock washer and remove the two gear selector quadrant bolts.
4 Lift out the gear lever shaft, selector mechanism, selector fork and pin, followed by the gear pinions and shafts.

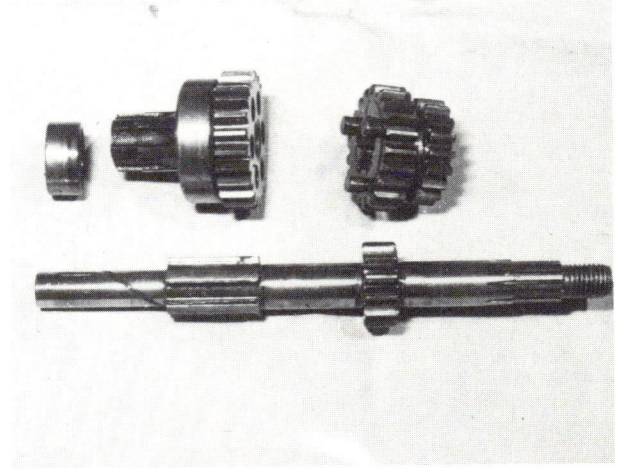

13.4 The mainshaft and gears

Chapter 1: Engine, clutch and gearbox

13.4a The layshaft and gears

14 Cylinder head - examination and renovation

1 It is unlikely that the cylinder head will require any special attention apart from removing the carbon deposit from the combustion chamber. Finish off with metal polish; a polished surface will reduce the tendency for carbon to adhere and will also help improve the gas flow.
2 Check that the cooling fins are not obstructed so that they receive the full air flow. A wire brush provides the best means of cleaning.
3 Check the condition of the thread where the spark plug is inserted. The thread in an aluminium alloy cylinder head is damaged very easily if the spark plug is overtightened. If necessary, the thread can be reclaimed by fitting what is known as a Helicoil insert. Most agents have facilities for this type of repair, which is not expensive.
4 If the cylinder head joint has shown signs of oil seepage when the machine was in use, check whether the cylinder head is distorted by laying it on a sheet of plate glass. Severe distortion will necessitate a replacement head but if the distortion is only slight it is permissible to wrap some emery cloth (fine grade) around the sheet of glass and rub down the joint using a rotary motion, until it is once again flat. The usual cause of distortion is uneven tightening of the cylinder head nuts.

15 Cylinder barrel - examination and renovation

1 There will probably be a lip at the uppermost end of the cylinder barrel, which marks the limit of travel of the top piston ring. The depth of the lip will give some indication of the amount of bore wear that has taken place, even though the amount of wear is not evenly distributed.
2 Remove the rings from the piston taking great care as they are brittle and very easily broken. There is more tendency for the rings to gum in their grooves in a two-stroke engine.
3 Measure the piston to bore clearance with a feeler gauge and compare with the wear limits given in the Specification Section of this Chapter. Rebore and fit an oversize piston, if necessary.
4 Give the cylinder barrel a close visual inspection. If the surface of the bore is scored or grooved, indicative of an earlier seizure or a displaced circlip and gudgeon pin, a rebore is essential. Compression loss will have a very marked effect on performance.
5 Check that the outside of the cylinder barrel is clean and free from road dirt. Use a wire brush on the cooling fins if they are obstructed in any way. The engine will overheat badly if the cooling area is obstructed in any way.
6 Clean all carbon deposits from the exhaust ports and try and obtain a smooth finish in the ports without in any way enlarging them or altering their shape. The size and position of the ports predetermines the characteristics of the engine and unwarranted tampering can produce very adverse effects. An enlarged or re-profiled port does not necessarily guarantee an increase in performance.

16 Piston and piston rings - examination and renovation

1 Attention to the piston and piston rings can be overlooked if a rebore is necessary because new replacements will be fitted.
2 If a rebore is not considered necessary, the piston should be examined closely. Reject the piston if it is badly scored or if it is badly discoloured as the result of the exhaust gases by-passing the rings.
3 Remove all carbon from the piston crown and use metal polish to finish off. Carbon will not adhere so readily to a polished surface.
4 Check that the gudgeon pin bosses are not worn or the circlip grooves damaged. Check also the piston ring pegs, to make sure that none has worked loose.
5 The grooves in which the piston rings locate can also become enlarged in use. The clearance between the piston and the ring in the groove should be checked with a feeler gauge (cf specification).
6 Piston ring wear can be checked by inserting the rings in the cylinder bore from the top and pushing them down about 1½ inches with the crown of the piston, so that they rest square in the cylinder. Measure the gap with a feeler gauge (cf specification).
7 Examine the working surface of the rings. If discoloured areas are evident, the rings should be replaced since the patches indicate the blow-by of gas. Check also that there is not a build-up of carbon behind the tapered ends of the rings, where they locate with the piston ring pegs.
8 It cannot be over-emphasised that the condition of the piston and rings in a two-stroke engine is of prime importance, especially since they control the opening and closing of the ports in the cylinder barrel by providing an effective seal. A two-stroke engine has only three working parts, one of which is the piston. It follows that the efficiency of the engine is very dependent on condition of this component and the parts with which it is closely associated.

17 Small end bearing - examination and renovation

1 The small-end bearing of a two-stroke engine is more prone to wear, producing the characteristic rattle that is heard in many engines that have covered a considerable mileage. The gudgeon pin should be a good sliding fit in the bearing, without evidence of any play. If play is apparent, the bearing must be renewed.
2 A plain phosphor bronze bush is fitted. The new bearing can be used to push the old bearing out of position by using a drawbolt and distance piece arrangement as shown in the accompanying diagram.
3 When the new bush is in position, it will be necessary to ream it out to the correct size, to offset the slight compression that has occurred when the bush was drawn into position. Only a very small amount of metal will need removing, otherwise the gudgeon pin fit will again be too slack.

18 Crankshaft assembly - examination and renovation

1 Wash the complete flywheel assembly with a petrol/paraffin mix to remove all surplus oil. Then hold the connecting rod at its highest point of travel (fully extended) and check whether there

Chapter 1: Engine, clutch and gearbox

is any vertical play in the big-end bearing by alternately pulling and pushing in the direction of travel. If the bearing is sound, there should be no play whatsoever, see Specifications.

2 Ignore any sideplay unless this appears to be excessive. A certain amount of play in this direction is necessary if the bottom end of the engine is to run freely, see Specifications.

3 Although it may be possible to run the engine for a further short period of service with a very small amount of play in the big-end bearing, this course of action is not advisable. Apart from the danger of the connecting rod breaking if the amount of wear increases rapidly, a further complete engine strip will be necessary to effect the renewal. It is best to replace the big-end bearing at this stage, if it is in any way suspect. Wear is denoted by the characteristic 'knock' when the engine is running under load.

4 Obtain a replacement flywheel assembly from an MZ agent. The only alternative is to separate the flywheels and fit a new big-end bearing; a highly specialised task that requires a press for separating the flywheels and a lathe for realigning the rebuilt assembly. This work is best entrusted to a qualified repairer, especially since the average owner will not have the necessary experience or access to the equipment needed.

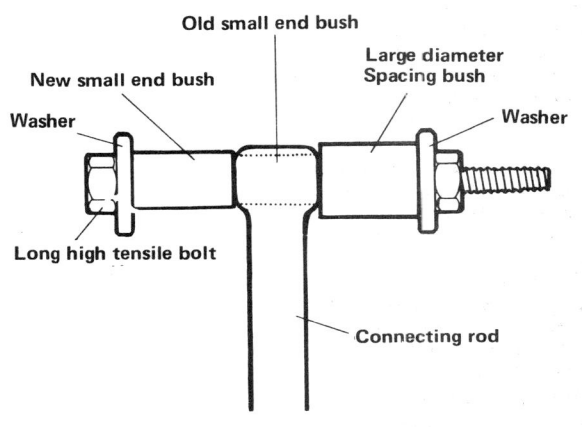

Fig. 1.2 Method for replacing small end bush

19 Main bearings and oil seals - examination

1 When the bearings have been pressed from their housings, wash them with a petrol/paraffin mix, to remove all traces of oil. If there is any play in the ball or roller bearings, or if they do not revolve smoothly, new replacements should be fitted.

2 It is highly desirable to replace the oil seals, particularly those fitted to the crankshaft. Worn oil seals will admit air to the crankcase of a two-stroke engine, which will dilute the incoming mixture whilst it is under crankcase compression. Crankcase air leaks are the most frequent cause of difficult starting and uneven running in any two-stroke engine.

20 Crankcases - examination and renovation

1 Inspect the crankcases for cracks or any other signs of damage. If a crack is found, specialist treatment will be required to effect a satisfactory repair.

2 Clean off the jointing faces, using a rag soaked in methylated spirit to remove old gasket cement. Do not use a scraper because the jointing surfaces are damaged very easily. A leak-tight crankcase is an essential requirement of any two-stroke engine. Check also the bearing housings, to make sure they are not damaged. The entry to the housings should be free from burrs or lips.

3 Do not forget to check also the dynamo cover and the primary drive cover.

21 Primary chain - examination and renewal

1 Although the primary chain runs in ideal conditions, where it is both enclosed and fully lubricated, inspection is necessary from time to time. No means of adjustment is provided; when the chain becomes too slack it has reached the point of renewal and must be replaced.

2 The chain is continuous and a spring link is fitted.

3 After a considerable period of service, it is probable that the sprockets will also need renewing. The usual indication occurs when a new primary chain is fitted which will tend to be too slack as the result of sprocket wear. When the sprockets have to be renewed, renew also the chain. It is bad practice to use an old chain with new sprockets - all should be renewed and run together at the same time. Note that MZ offer a selection of four chains, to accommodate sprocket wear of up to 0.3 mm (0.010 in.).

22 Clutch assembly - examination and renovation

1 Examine the condition of the linings of the inserted clutch plates. If they are damaged, loose or have worn thin, replacements will be required. Measure the thickness of the linings and compare with the Specifications Section of this Chapter.

2 Examine the tongues of the plain clutch plates, where they engage with the clutch drum. After an extended period of service, burrs will form on the edges of the tongues which will correspond with grooves worn in the clutch drum slots. These burrs must be removed, by dressing with a smooth file.

3 The grooves worn in the clutch drum slots can be dressed in a similar manner, making sure that the edges of the slots are square once again. If this simple operation is overlooked, clutch troubles will persist because the plates tend to lodge in the grooves when the clutch is withdrawn and promote clutch drag.

4 Check also the condition of the clutch springs.

23 Gearbox components - examination and renovation

1 Examine carefully the gearbox components for signs of wear or damage such as chipped or broken teeth on the gear pinions and kickstart quadrant, rounded dogs on the ends of the gear pinions, bent selector forks, weakened or damaged springs and worn splines. If there is any doubt about the condition of a part, it is preferable to play safe and replace the part at this stage. Remember that if a suspect part should fail later, it will be necessary to completely strip the engine/gearbox unit again.

2 Do not forget to examine the kickstart ratchet assembly. Examination will show whether the ratchet teeth have worn, causing the kickstart to slip.

3 All the gear dogs should have a slight undercut (5°). If this has been reduced by wear the machine will jump out of gear. Renew the gears only as a pair.

4 Note that the splines on the 150 model gearboxes have machined cutaways.

24 Reassembling the engine/gearbox unit - general

1 Again the importance of cleanliness cannot be overstressed. All components should be clean and lightly oiled. All bearings should be pre-lubricated.

2 Renew all gaskets and 'O' rings. When replacing oil seals it is a good idea to lightly grease their lips with a molybdenum disulphide or graphited grease to stop seizure and consequential premature failure.

3 All old gaskets should be removed and the jointing faces cleaned with a solvent such as methylated spirits to remove the old gasket cement.

4 Make sure you have all the necessary gaskets, 'O' rings and circlips etc. before starting the rebuild. Always fit new piston circlips.
5 Clean all tools before starting the rebuild to stop the grit that accumulates on them from entering the engine. This practice is frequently overlooked.

25 Reassembing the engine/gearbox unit - fitting bearings and oil seals into crankcase

1 Refit the bearings into the crankcase halves. It is preferable to heat the crankcase to 100°C in an oven and then drop the bearing into position. If a drift is used to replace the bearings, make sure it bears only on the outside ring of the bearing; a socket will often suffice as a drift. Note that integral oil seals are fitted to the gearbox shaft bearings.
2 Replace the oil seals by carefully drifting them into position. Lubricate the lips of the oil seals with a little graphited or molybdenum grease. Good crankcase seals are essential to the efficient running of any two-stroke engine and if there is any doubt about the condition of the old seals they should be replaced without hesitation. Poor starting and indifferent running can often be attributed to worn or damaged oil seals, that allow air to enter the crankcase and dilute the incoming mixture whilst it is under crankcase compression.
3 Do not omit the circlips that retain the bearings in position.

26 Reassembling the engine/gearbox unit - replacing the gears and selector

1 Assemble the gear selector fork and pin and the selector quadrant.
2 Place the gear lever shaft and selector quadrant in the crankcase.
3 Engage the fork of the gear quadrant on the selector fork and screw in the pin. Replace the two quadrant bolts and knock over the tabs on the lockwashers. Insert the mainshaft and sliding gear into the bearing making sure to locate the selector fork between the two gears.
4 Place the large gear from the layshaft, flat side up, in the crankcase over the bearing.
5 Assemble the two layshaft sliding gears and locate them in the selector fork, smaller gear on top.
6 Insert the layshaft, making sure not to disturb the other gears.
7 Replace the gearbox sleeve gear, bearing, and collar, on the mainshaft.
8 Replace the selector fork pin, lockwasher and nut, but do not tighten at this stage.

27 Reassembling the engine/gearbox unit - adjusting and setting the gear selector mechanism

1 The gear selector pin and fork also act as the positive stop mechanism when selecting gears. The pin is grooved and the position of these grooves determines the movement of the sliding gears. Adjustment of the groove height is made by screwing the pin either up or down.
2 Select top gear and check that the gearbox shafts are fully home in their bearings. Check the clearance between the top two gears on the mainshaft with a feeler gauge (see Fig. 1.3). Engage third gear and check the clearance between the fixed gear and sliding gear with a pair of dividers or vernier caliper (see Fig. 1.3). Screw the selector pin to obtain the correct clearances. Tighten the locknut and check the clearances again. If correct, knock over the tab on the lockwasher. If the setting has moved, readjust as necessary. Make sure that the lockwasher does not obstruct the adjacent screw hole.

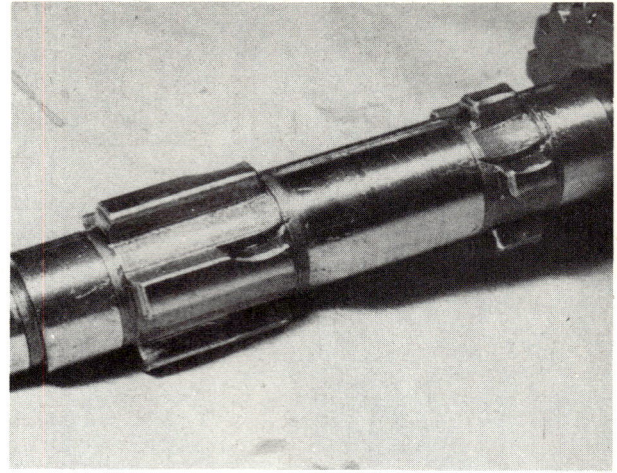

23.4 Note the spline cutaways

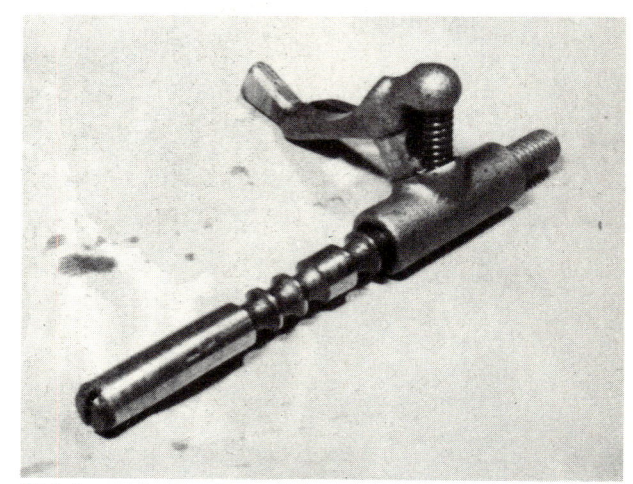

26.1 Assemble the selector fork and pin and ...

26.1a ... the gear selector quadrant

26.2 Replace and engage the quadrant and gear lever shaft

26.3 Engage and replace the selector fork and pin

26.3a Knock over the tab on the lockwashers

26.3b Insert the mainshaft and sliding gear engaging the selector fork

26.4 Replace the large layshaft gear

26.5 Assemble and engage the sliding gears in the selector fork

26.6 Slide in the layshaft

26.7 Replace gearbox sprocket gear, bearing and collar

26.8 Replace, but do not tighten, the selector fork pin locknut

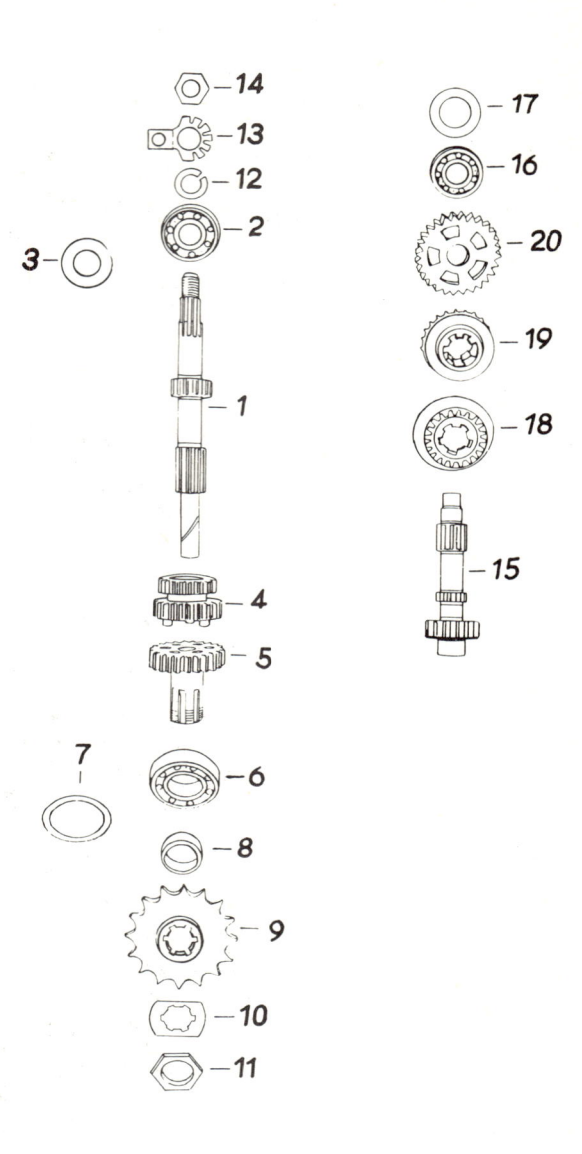

Fig. 1.3 TS150 gearbox components

1 Mainshaft
2 Main bearing (mainshaft)
3 Spacer
4 Mainshaft sliding 2nd and 4th gear
5 Mainshaft top gear, with bush
6 Main bearing (mainshaft)
7 Spacer
8 Spacer for sprocket
9 Final drive sprocket (15 or 16 teeth)
10 Locking plate
11 Sprocket retaining nut
12 Spring washer
13 Tab washer
14 Hexagon nut
15 Layshaft
16 Main bearing (layshaft)
17 Oil thrower
18 Layshaft sliding 3rd gear
19 Layshaft sliding 1st gear
20 1st gear pinion

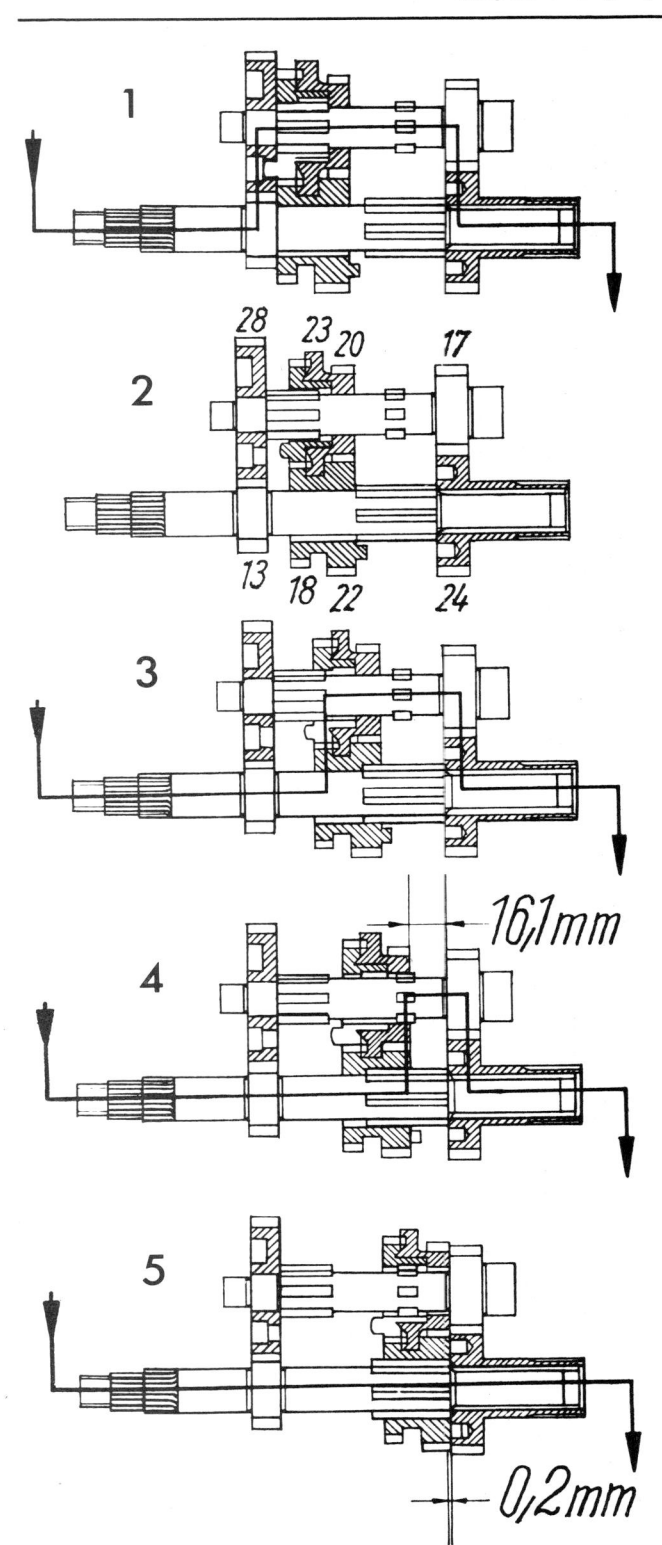

Chapter 1: Engine, clutch and gearbox 23

27.2 Check the gear clearance with a feeler gauge and ...

27.2a ... caliper

Fig. 1.4 Gearbox drive train and setting tolerances

1 Bottom gear
2 Neutral
3 Second gear
4 Third gear
5 Top gear

28 Reassembling the engine/gearbox unit - replacing the crankshaft and joining the crankcase

1 Fit the crankshaft assembly in the left-hand crankcase.
2 Check that the gasket faces are clean and apply a proprietary jointing compound (no gasket is used).
3 Fit the right-hand crankcase carefully, using a soft faced hammer.
4 Knock in the two hollow dowels.
5 Check that the crankshaft rotates freely. If it does not, try gently tapping either it or the bearing. Proper location of the crankshaft without radial pressure on the ball races is imperative if premature bearing failure is to be avoided.
6 Replace the crankcase screws and tighten them in an even and diagonal sequence.
7 Again, check that the crankshaft rotates freely and that all gears can be selected.
8 Check that the gearbox breather hole, located behind the crankcase mouth, is clear and not blocked with jointing compound.

Chapter 1: Engine, clutch and gearbox

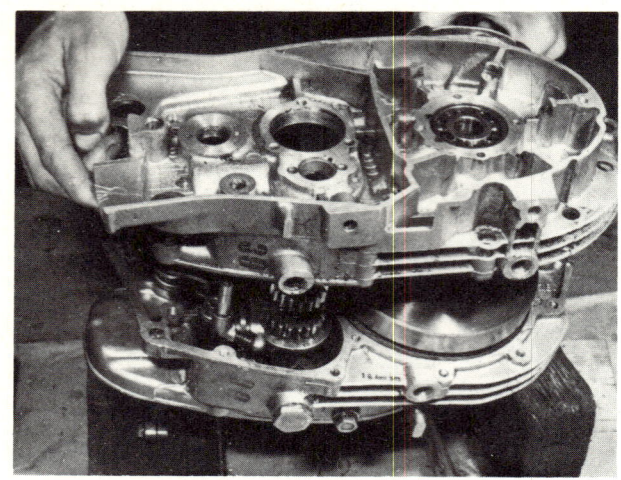

28.3 Replace the right-hand crankcase

28.4 Knock in the rear and ...

28.4a ... front hollow dowels

29 Reassembling the engine/gearbox unit - replacing the right-hand external oil seals

1 Grease the lip of the oil seals with a little graphited or molybdenum grease before replacing them. Use new gaskets.
2 Replace the crankshaft oil seal cup* and tighten the four screws evenly and in a diagonal sequence.
3 Replace the gearbox oil seal cup and evenly tighten the five screws in a diagonal sequence.
*N.B. If the main bearings have been disturbed and/or the crankshaft renewed it is necessary to check the clearance between the oil seal cup and the face of the bearing with a feeler gauge (see Fig. 1.4). The clearance should be adjusted to 0.4 mm (0.016 in.) by shims. Do not forget to take into account the gasket thickness of approximately 0.1 mm (0.004 in.)

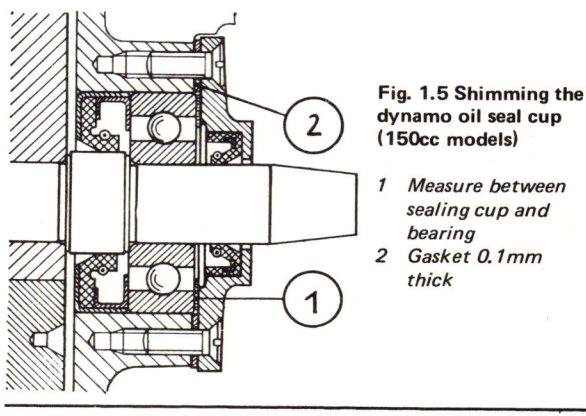

Fig. 1.5 Shimming the dynamo oil seal cup (150cc models)

1 Measure between sealing cup and bearing
2 Gasket 0.1mm thick

30 Reassembling the engine/gearbox unit - replacing the kickstart mechanism

1 Replace the kickstart ratchet gear on the clutch drum followed by the spring, spring cap and wire circlip.
2 Fit the thrust washer to the kickstart shaft and quadrant and replace the assembly in the crankcase. Locate the end of the clock spring in the crankcase lug and tension the shaft one complete turn.

31 Reassembling the engine/gearbox unit - replacing the primary drive and clutch

1 Fit the Woodruff key in the crankshaft. Make sure that the taper is clean, also the mating taper in the engine sprocket.
2 Replace the thrust washer and bearing on the gearbox mainshaft.
3 Temporarily replace the engine sprocket and clutch drum. Check that they are in line, by placing a straight edge on top of the sprockets. Shim behind the clutch drum if adjustment is necessary. Remove the engine sprocket and clutch drum and assemble them with the chain. Replace them as a complete unit.
4 Replace the engine sprocket washer and nut. Lock the engine as described in Section 5 of this Chapter and tighten the nut.
5 Replace the clutch centre, lockwasher and nut and tighten the nut. This has a **left-hand** thread. Knock back the tab on the lockwasher.
6 Replace the clutch backplate with the chamfered edge downwards, followed by alternate friction and plain plates.
7 Grease and replace the clutch mushroom and fit the pressure plate.
8 Replace the six spring cups, springs and locating collars.
9 Compress the springs and replace the fixing pins (see Section 11.1 of this Chapter for the method used to compress the springs).
10 Replace the thrust washer on the kickstart lever shaft.

29.2 Replace the crankshaft and ...

29.3 ... gearbox oil seal cups. Do not forget the shims

30.2 Replace the thrust washer

31.1 Fit the Woodruff key

31.2 Replace the thrust washer and bearing

31.5 Replace the lockwasher and ...

31.5a ... tighten the nut - left-hand thread

31.6 Replace back plate, chamfer downwards, followed by ...

31.6a ... alternate friction and plain plates

31.7 Do not forget the clutch mushroom before ...

31.7a ... replacing the pressure plate

31.10 Do not forget the kickstart shaft thrust washer

Chapter 1: Engine, clutch and gearbox

32 Reassembling the engine/gearbox unit - replacing the left-hand engine cover

1 Renew the kickstart/gear lever shaft rubber 'O' ring located in the left-hand cover.
2 Clean the gasket faces and fit a new gasket.
3 Replace the left-hand cover and tighten the four screws. Do not overtighten the two front screws.

33 Reassembling the engine/gearbox unit - replacing the gearbox final drive sprocket

1 Replace the gearbox sprocket, belled side up, lockwasher and nut.
2 Tighten the nut, which has a **left-hand** thread. This can be accomplished by either locking the engine, as described in Section 5 of this Chapter and placing it in gear, or by using the rear chain to jam the sprocket.
3 Grease and replace the clutch operating pushrod.

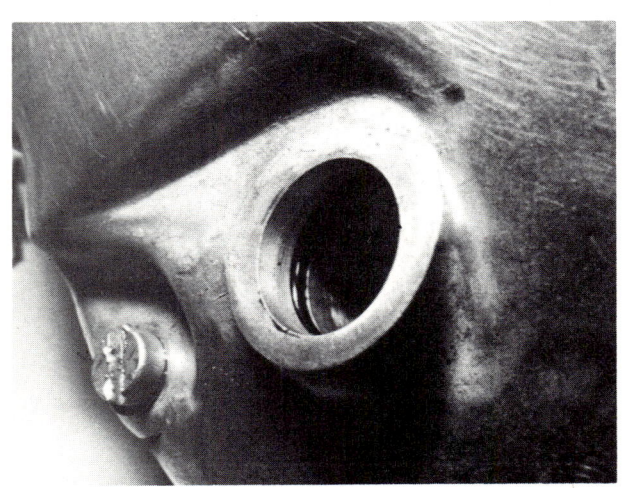

33.2 Jam sprocket to tighten the left-hand thread nut

34 Reassembling the engine/gearbox unit - replacing the dynamo, neutral light switch and exhaust mounting brackets

1 Fit the Woodruff key to crankshaft. Clean the taper and replace the dynamo armature and contact breaker cam. Make sure that the slot in the contact breaker cam locates on the peg of the armature. Replace the armature bolt and tighten.
2 Replace the dynamo outer. Make sure that the slot aligns with the peg in the crankcase. Replace and tighten the two retaining screws.
3 Replace the two carbon brushes.
4 See Chapter 3 for the methods used to time the ignition and the contact breaker.
5 Replace the neutral light switch after gaping the contacts within the range, 0.6 - 0.8 mm (0.024 - 0.031 in.). Do not tighten the two retaining screws since it will be necessary to adjust the switch when the engine is installed in the frame.
6 Replace the two exhaust mounting brackets.

32.1 Renew the rubber O-ring in the left-hand cover

33.1 The gearbox sprocket is fitted belled side up

34.1 Fit the Woodruff key

34.2 Slot in dynamo outer locates over pin in crankcase

34.3 Replace the carbon brushes and springs

34.5 Fit the neutral light switch

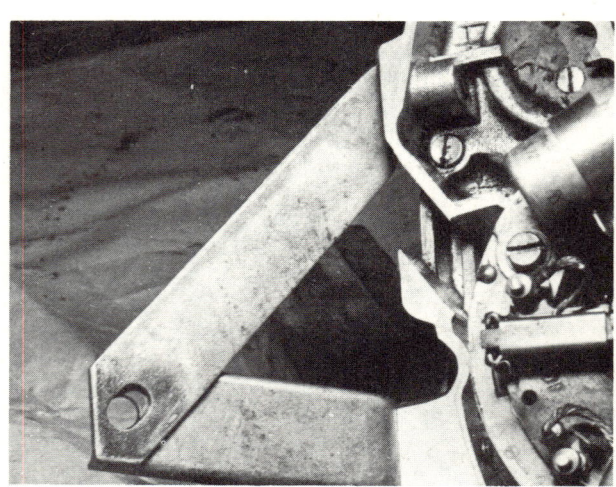

34.6 Replace the two exhaust mounting brackets

35 Reassembling the engine/gearbox unit - replacing the piston, cylinder barrel and head

1 Refit the piston rings after having checked their end gaps, (see Specifications). Locate each ring gap over the peg in the piston groove, to prevent the rings from turning.
2 Replace one of the piston circlips. Always use new circlips. Make sure that the circlip is seated in its groove correctly.
3 Oil the small end bearing.
4 If the gudgeon pin is a tight fit in the piston, pre-heat the piston in some hot water to facilitate refitting the pin.
5 Place the piston over the connecting rod the correct way round (with the arrow on the piston pointing forwards towards the exhaust port) and insert the gudgeon pin. Replace the other piston circlip, making sure it is seated properly.
6 Fit a new cylinder base gasket. Make sure that the gasket does not protrude into the transfer ports. Cut to shape with scissors, if necessary.
7 Oil the piston rings and check that they are still correctly positioned. Remove any rag that may have been placed in the crankcase mouth.
8 Slide the cylinder barrel down the studs over the piston and rings whilst compressing the latter with your fingers. Push the barrel right home. If it is tight, loosen the two screws at each side of the crankcase mouth. Do not forget to retighten both screws afterwards.
9 If the engine has an inclined spark plug and has to be retimed, do not fit the cylinder head yet. It is necessary to set the ignition timing as described in Chapter 3.
10 Check the head and barrel joint faces are clean. Replace the cylinder head. No head gasket is fitted and no jointing compound is necessary.
11 Tighten down the cylinder head nuts evenly and diagonally to a torque wrench setting of 30 lb ft.
12 Check that the gearbox breather hole located behind the crankcase mouth is clear and not blocked with jointing compound.

36 Reassembling the engine/gearbox unit - refitting the engine in the frame, adjustment of neutral light switch and clutch

1 Engine replacement is a reversal of the procedure described in Section 3 of this Chapter. However, before replacing the right-hand engine cover, it is necessary to adjust the neutral light

Chapter 1: Engine, clutch and gearbox

35.5 Arrow on piston must point forwards when ...

35.5a ... the piston is fitted

35.8 Slide the barrel over the piston

35.8a If the barrel is tight fit loosen crankcase screws

35.12 Check breather is clear

switch. With all the electrics connected, the ignition switch on and the gearbox in neutral, rotate the switch until the gearbox indicator lamp is lit. Tighten the two screws. Check that the bulb is still lit and that it goes out when a gear is selected. Readjust as necessary.

2 Grease and replace the clutch operating worm complete with return spring. Make sure that the ball bearing is located within the operating worm. Replace the cover and retighten the two screws.

3 Slacken the clutch adjuster screw locknut. Rotate the adjuster screw clockwise until pressure is just felt. Back the screw off three-quarters of a turn and tighten the locknut. Recheck the adjustment.

37 Starting and running the rebuilt engine

1 Make sure everything has been replaced, reconnected and tightened. Check the oil and petrol levels. Make sure the bike is not in gear and that the engine turns over freely, but has compression when the kickstart is depressed.

2 Turn on the petrol and allow a few moments for it to flow into the carburettor. Start in the usual manner. Do not rev the engine at first.

36.4 Hold screw when tightening lock nut

36.5 Use new exhaust pipe gasket

3 Check the engine for blowing gaskets, oil and petrol leaks. Check that all the controls are functioning properly, ie; gears, clutch, lights and most important, the brakes.

4 Any rebuilt machine requires a little time to settle down and for the usual performance to be obtained. Do not overwork the engine until it has bedded down.

5 If the engine has been rebored and/or a new crankshaft fitted, the engine will have to be run-in, observing the usual running-in procedure.

6 If anything seems to be wrong or there are any peculiar noises, stop the machine immediately and investigate.

7 After the machine has been run for a little time, retighten the cylinder head nuts and check the various settings.

38 Fault diagnosis - engine

Refer to Section 79 of this Chapter.

39 Fault diagnosis - gearbox

Refer to Section 80 of this Chapter.

40 Fault diagnosis - clutch

Refer to Section 81 of this Chapter.

Chapter 1: Engine, clutch and gearbox

250 cc models

41 General description

The ES and TS250 models use basically the same engine, the difference in power output being obtained by altering the timing and shape of the ports. The engines are air-cooled, single cylinder two-strokes, utilising a loop scavenging system. Lubrication for the engine is provided by a petroil mixture. The gearbox and clutch have their own integral oil supply.

The crankshaft runs in two large diameter ball journal bearings, while the connecting rod is fitted with a roller bearing big-end and a double needle roller small-end. Crankshaft endfloat is controlled by shims.

The clutch is mounted directly on the crankshaft and thus runs at engine speed. Primary drive to the four-speed gearbox is by helically cut gears.

The electrical system is 6 volt. The dynamo armature is directly mounted on the right-hand end of the crankshaft.

42 Operations with engine in the frame

Refer to Section 2 of this Chapter.

43 Removing the engine/gearbox unit

1 Place the machine on the centre stand and make sure it is standing firmly on level ground.
2 Remove the oil drain plug (see Chapter 2, Section 11, for location) and allow the oil to drain into a suitable receptacle.
3 Remove the petrol pipe from the tap.
4 Remove the carburettor shield (where applicable) which is retained by one central screw. Remove the rubber hose connecting the carburettor to the air filter.
5 Unscrew the cold start device from the carburettor and hook it up in a safe place. Unscrew the ring nut, pull out the throttle slide and hook it up safely.
6 Disconnect the battery leads from the battery, which is located behind the left-hand side panel.
7 Remove the exhaust system complete by undoing the rear stay bolt, the rubber mounting at the joint and the exhaust nut on the cylinder barrel.
8 Remove the two dynamo cover screws (right-hand side) and lift off the cover.
9 Disconnect the four leads going to the dynamo, making a note of where each lead is connected. Remove the spark plug cap.
10 Pull the chain gaiters away from the engine and disconnect the rear chain at the spring link.
11 Unscrew the clutch cable holder from the left-hand side cover and unhook the cable.

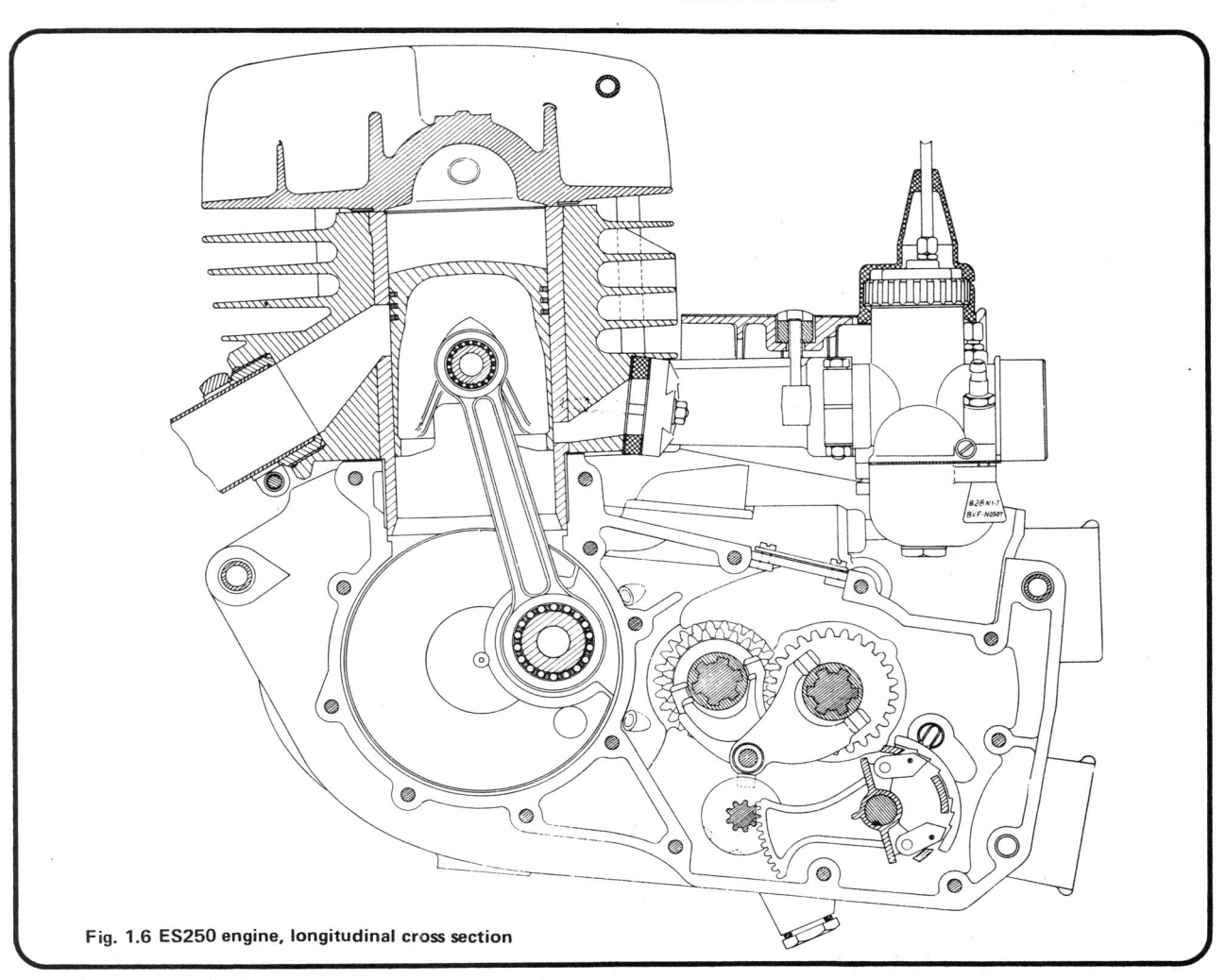

Fig. 1.6 ES250 engine, longitudinal cross section

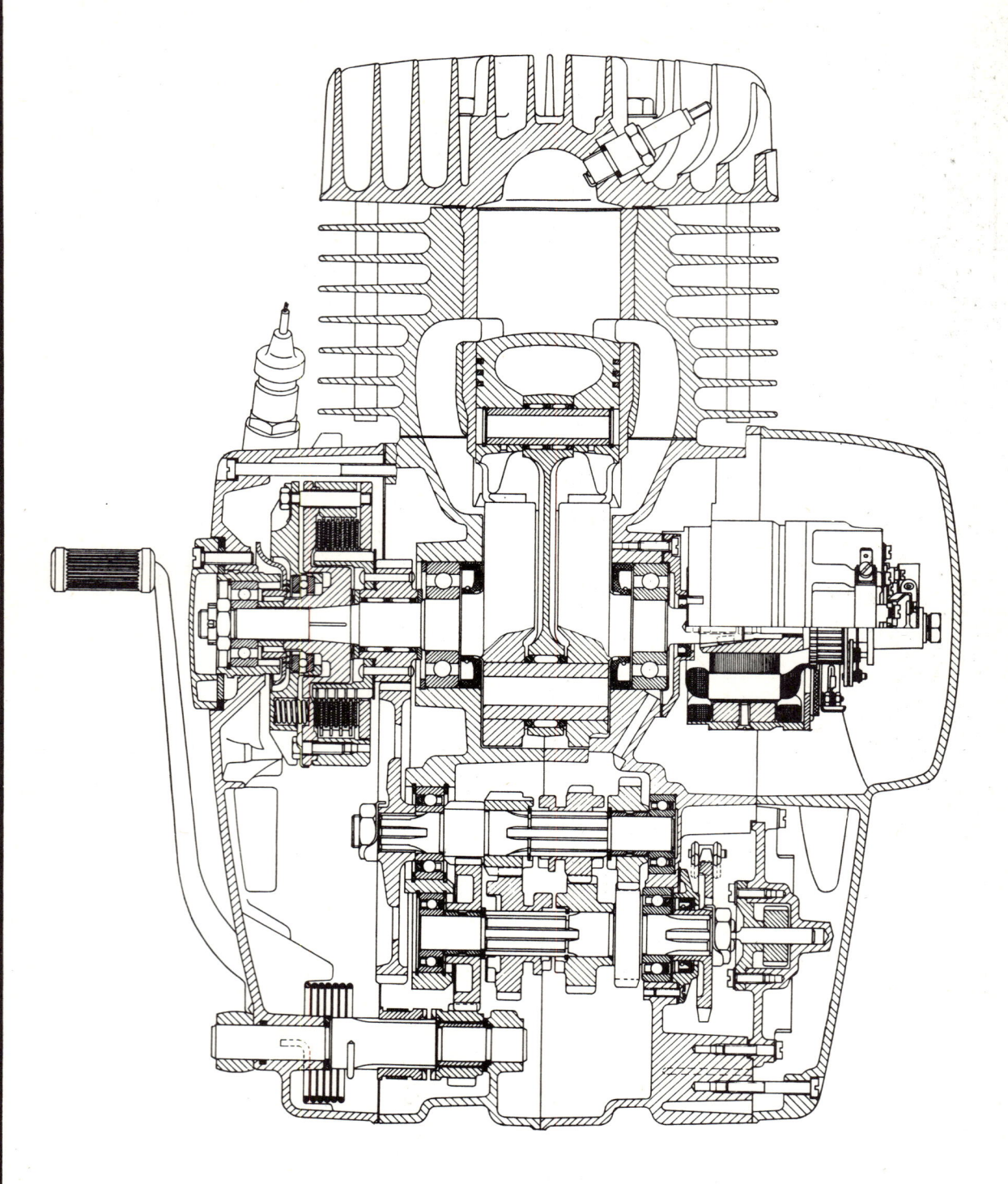

Fig. 1.7 ES250 engine cross section

Chapter 1: Engine, clutch and gearbox

ES250

12 Remove the three screws holding the speedometer drive gearbox and lift the unit clear from the sprocket. Unscrew the speedometer cable and pull it out from the gearbox unit. To dismantle the speedometer drive gearbox, see Chapter 5, Section 14.3.

13 Hinge the seat sideways and remove the two bolts located at the rear of the petrol tank. Lift off the petrol tank.

14 If leg shields are fitted, they should be removed.

15 Remove the horn from its bracket by undoing the nut at the rear.

16 Unhook the prop stand spring and remove the two rear engine mounting bolts.

17 Slacken the nuts on the Silentbloc engine mounting, one each side. The engine is now free to be lifted out from the frame. Before removing the engine, check that all the necessary cables and wiring have been disconnected.

TS250

18 Support the engine with a wooden block and remove the two engine mounting nuts at the rear of the cylinder head.

19 Remove the two rear engine bolts. The engine is now free to be lifted away from the frame. Before removing the engine, check that all the necessary cables and wiring have been disconnected.

43.4 Remove the carburettor shield

43.5 Unscrew the cold start plunger and ...

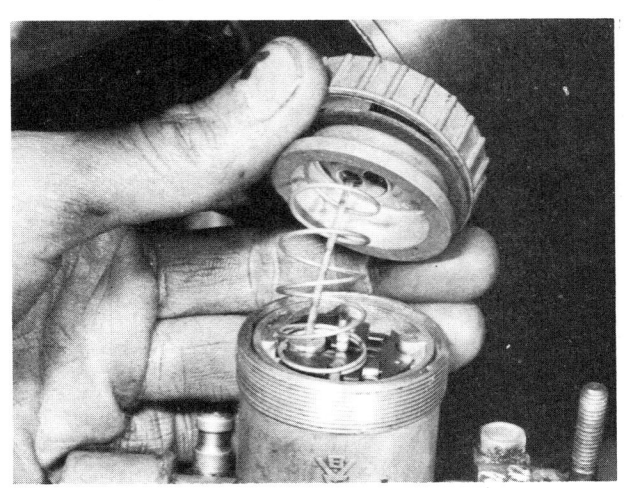

43.5a ... carburettor top

43.8 Lift off the right-hand cover

43.9 Disconnect dynamo wires, noting their position

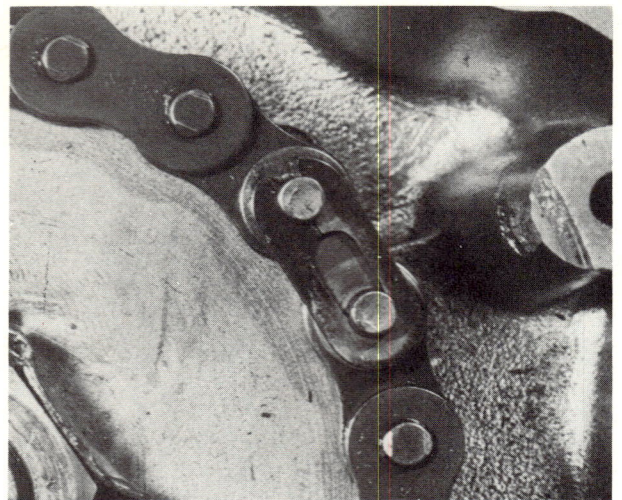

43.10 Disconnect the chain at spring link

43.11 Unscrew and disconnect clutch cable

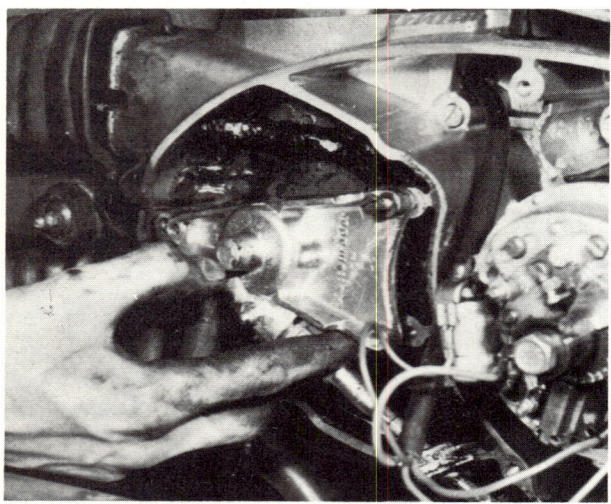

43.12 Remove speedometer drive gearbox retaining screw and ...

43.12a ... disconnect the cable

43.15 The horn has to be removed

43.16 Remove the rear engine mounting bolts and ...

Chapter 1: Engine, clutch and gearbox

43.17 ... bottom Silentbloc nuts

44 Dismantling the engine/gearbox unit - general

Refer to Section 4 of this Chapter.

45 Preventing the engine from turning for dismantling and reassembly purposes

Refer to Section 5 of this Chapter.

46 Dismantling the engine/gearbox unit - removing the cylinder head, barrel and piston

1 Remove the four cylinder head nuts in a diagonal sequence to avoid distorting the head. Lift the head off the studs.
2 Slide the barrel off the studs, whilst supporting the piston to prevent it or the rings from damage. If the barrel is tight, slacken off the nut at the top of the crankcase mouth behind the cylinder barrel.
3 It is advisable to stuff the open crankcase mouth with rag to stop anything falling in, and also to prevent damage by the connecting rod striking the crankcase.
4 Remove the circlips from the piston and press out the gudgeon pin. If the pin is a tight fit, gently heat the piston; a rag soaked in boiling water should suffice. Place the piston and double row needle roller small-end bearing on one side. The needles should be retained in the bearing. If they fall out, discard the bearing and obtain a new one.

47 Dismantling the engine/gearbox unit - removing gearbox sprocket and engine mounting strap

1 Knock back the tab on the locking washer and undo the gearbox sprocket nut, whilst the engine is locked, by putting it into gear and holding it as described in Section 45.
2 Lift off the sprocket and tab washer from the splined shaft.
3 Remove the engine mounting strap by undoing the two retaining bolts (ES250 models).

48 Dismantling the engine/gearbox unit - removing the dynamo

1 Undo the two screws that retain the dynamo outer and lift the unit out. Be careful not to damage the resistor coil when handling the unit.
2 Lock the engine as described in Section 45.
3 Undo the dynamo armature bolt. Remove the contact breaker cam. The armature is held in position by a roller key in a tapered shaft. If an extractor is not available, use the front crankcase clamp bolt together with a short spacer (a length of 6 mm bolt) as an extractor. Screw this into the armature until pressure is felt, then smartly hit the end of the bolt to release the armature from the tapered shaft.
4 Remove the roller key from the tapered shaft.

49 Dismantling the engine/gearbox unit - removing the left-hand engine cover

1 Remove the bolt from the gear lever and pull the lever off its splined shaft.
2 Remove the three screws retaining the clutch adjuster cover plate and lift off the plate.
3 Lift out the adjusting ring and rubber 'O' ring.
4 Remove the split pin and undo the castellated nut.
5 Remove the five screws that retain the left-hand side cover (the sixth screw is an oil level) and lift the cover off. The cover will probably be tight and will require the cautious use of a soft-faced hammer. On no account use a screwdriver to lever the cover off since this will cause damage to the jointing faces.

50 Dismantling the engine/gearbox unit - removing the kickstart mechanism

1 Remove the cotter pin from the kickstart lever and pull the lever off its shaft. Be careful during this operation since the shaft is under spring tension.
2 The kickstart mechanism can now be withdrawn from the left-hand cover. Dismantle by firstly removing the wire circlip and then slide the components off the shaft.

51 Dismantling the engine/gearbox unit - removing the clutch and primary drive

1 Knock down the tab on the lockwasher on the large diameter primary drive gear and remove the nut.
2 The clutch is held onto the crankshaft by a taper. To remove it, a two or three jaw universal puller is required. When using the puller it is a good idea to replace the castle nut on the end of the crankshaft, to prevent the thread being damaged.
3 Lift off the small primary drive gear, noting the spring washer and thrust washer on top and the washer underneath the gear. The double needle roller bearing should also be removed.
4 Use the universal puller to remove the large diameter primary drive gear.
5 To strip the clutch further in order to gain access to the clutch plates, knock back the tabs on the lockwashers and undo the nuts evenly. Be careful, since the whole unit is under pressure from the clutch springs. Note the 'x' alignment marks on the main individual clutch components.

52 Dismantling the engine/gearbox unit - removing the oil seal cups

1 Undo the four screws and lift off the oil seal cup from the final drive gearbox shaft. Note the number of shims, if fitted.
2 Undo the six screws and lift off the oil seal cup from the crankshaft. Again note the number of shims, where fitted, and also the position of the cup since it has asymetrical oil channels.

46.4 Push out the gudgeon pin

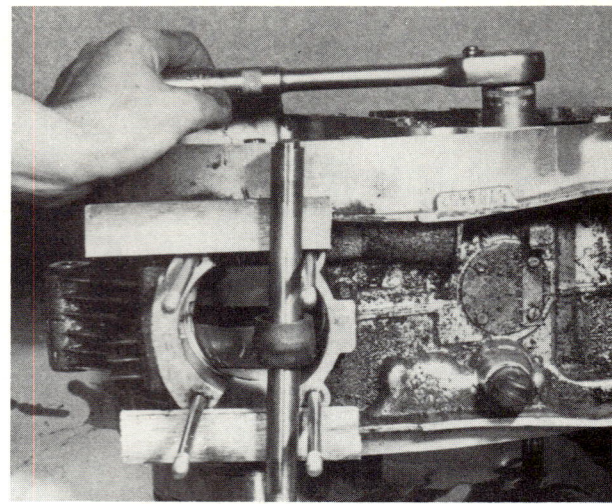

47.1 Method used to lock engine whilst removing gearbox sprocket nut

48.3 Use bolt and spacer to extract dynamo armature

48.4 Roller key is fitted to crankshaft taper

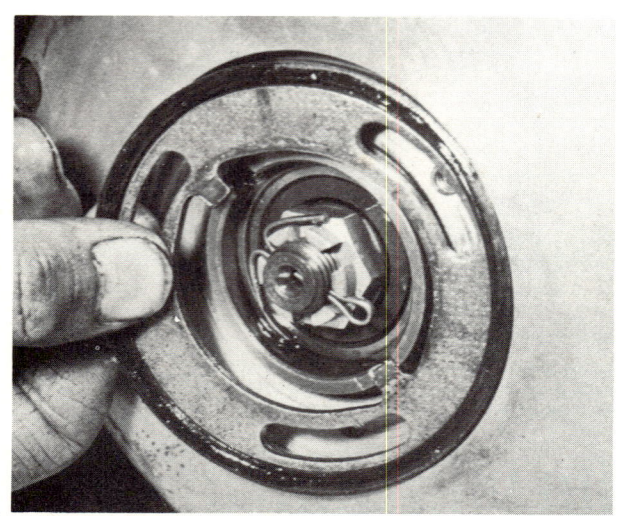

49.3 Lift out clutch adjusting plate

49.4 Remove split pin and undo castellated nut

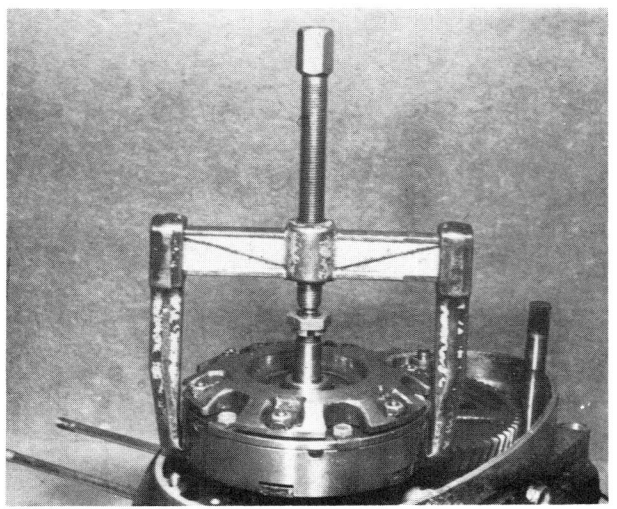

51.2 Puller is required to remove clutch. Note use of the nut to prevent damage to thread

51.3 A belled spring washer is fitted on top of the thrust washer

51.3a Thrust washer is fitted below primary drive gear

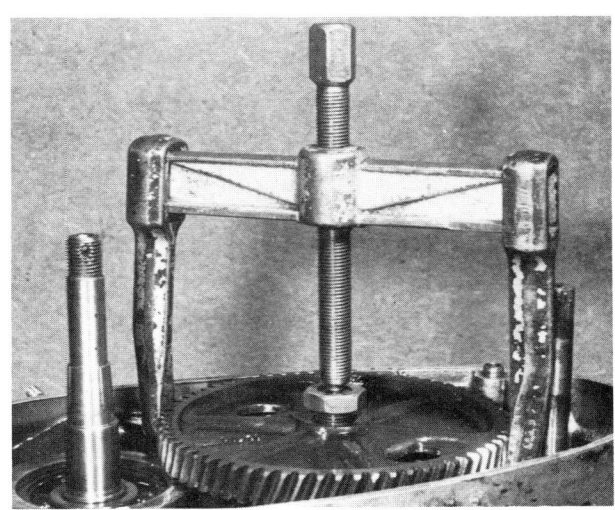

51.4 Use puller to remove large primary drive gear

52.1 Note shims behind the gearbox oil seal cup and ...

52.2 ... crankshaft cup

53 Dismantling the engine/gearbox unit - separating the crankcase

1 Remove the front engine bolt if this has not already been done and drift out the hollow dowel from the crankcase.
2 Remove the three rubber plugs from the right-hand crankcase half and undo the fifteen crankcase screws, also the nut at the top of the crankcase mouth.
3 Remove the four screws holding the circular steel cover on top of the crankcase and lift off the cover.
4 The crankcase is now ready to be parted. It will probably be very difficult to part but a soft faced hammer can be used cautiously, if necessary. When parted, the gearbox and crankshaft should remain in the left-hand crankcase. Note whether any shims are fitted and also the arrangement of the thrust washers in the gearbox. Do not use a screwdriver to separate the crankcase since it will inevitably damage the jointing faces.

53.2 Three crankcase screws are located behind rubber plugs

54 Dismantling the engine/gearbox unit - removing the crankshaft and gearbox components

1 Remove the crankshaft assembly from the left-hand crankcase.
2 Remove the gear selector stop ball and spring by unscrewing the bolt located underneath the crankcase (early models have two).
3 Lift out the gear selector shaft complete with quadrant and mechanism.
4 Lift out the selector fork pivot pin followed by both the selector forks and selector drum.
5 Remove both the gearbox shafts. Again, these can sometimes be tight.
6 The gearbox shafts can be dismantled further by sliding the gears off the shafts. Note the position of the thrust washers. Both shafts are made with one integral gear and the gear next to this is retained in position by a circlip.
7 The gear selector mechanism is dismantled by sliding the components off the shaft.

55 Cylinder head - examination and renovation

Refer to Section 14 of this Chapter.

56 Cylinder barrel - examination and renovation

Refer to Section 15 of this Chapter.

57 Piston and piston rings - examination and renovation

Refer to Section 16 of this Chapter.

58 Small end bearing - examination and replacement

1 There should be no perceptible play in the small-end needle roller bearing, see Fig. 1.8 for axial clearances.
2 On assembly the needle rollers are matched to the connecting rod eye and gudgeon pin. Since the tolerances are very small and extremely sophisticated, measuring equipment is required to measure the components, the job of matching the small-end, gudgeon pin and needle rollers is best left to an MZ agent.

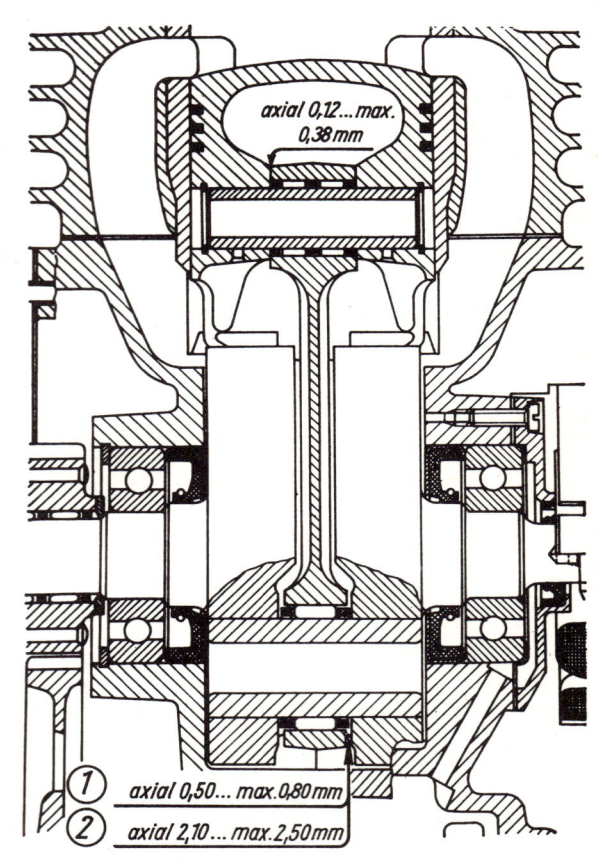

Fig. 1.8 Big and small end axial clearances

1 Axial clearance between needle bearing cage and crankshaft disc
2 Axial clearance between connecting rod and disc crankshaft

59 Crankshaft assembly - examination and renovation

1 For clearances see Fig. 1.8 and also refer to Section 18.

60 Main bearings and oil seals - examination

Refer to Section 19 of this Chapter.

Chapter 1: Engine, clutch and gearbox

61 Crankcase - examination and renovation

Refer to Section 20 of this Chapter.

62 Clutch assembly - examination and renovation

Refer to Section 22 of this Chapter.

63 Gearbox components - examination and renovation

Refer to Section 23 of this Chapter.

64 Engine mountings - examination and replacement

1 Examine the engine mounting rubbers for signs of deterioration. Particularly check the metal to rubber adhesion on the bottom Silentbloc mounting. Renew as necessary.
2 Refer to Chapter 4, Section 10.3 for details of rear engine mountings.

65 Reassembly - general

Refer to Section 24 of this Chapter.

66 Reassembling the engine/gearbox unit - fitting bearings and oil seals into crankcase

Refer to Section 25 of this Chapter.

67 Reassembling the engine/gearbox unit - replacing gears and selector drum

1 If the oil guide has been removed, replace it and do not forget to knock back the tab on the lockwasher.
2 Assemble the gears on their appropriate shafts and replace them as a unit in the left-hand crankcase.
3 Place the bottom selector fork pivot pin thrust washer in the crankcase and fit the selector forks to the gears. Note that the selector forks are different.
4 Replace the selector drum, making sure to locate the selector forks in their respective grooves.
5 Slide in the selector fork pivot pin. Replace the top thrust washer.
6 Replace the selector stop ball and spring and tighten the bolt.

68 Reassembling the engine/gearbox unit - replacing the gear selector mechanism

1 Reassemble the gear selector quadrant making sure that the dog springs are properly located.
2 Replace the hairpin gear lever return spring.
3 Slide the gear lever shaft and mechanism into the crankcase and locate it in its holder, aligning the dot on the quadrant with the chamfered tooth on the selector drum.
4 Replace the selector drum thrust washer.
5 Bend the neutral light switch wiper so that it is at a height of 5.5 mm (0.21 in.) above the top of the quadrant.

69 Reassembling the engine/gearbox unit - replacing the crankshaft and joining the crankcase

1 Fit the crankshaft assembly into the left-hand crankcase.
2 Check that the jointing faces are clean and apply a proprietary jointing compound (no gasket is used).
3 Fit the right-hand crankcase carefully, using a soft faced hammer. The fitting is made easier if the right-hand crankcase is pre-heated to about 80°C, causing expansion of the bearings and permitting an easier fit.
4 Knock in the front hollow locating dowel.
5 Check that the crankshaft rotates freely. If it does not, try tapping it gently on the bearing in the right-hand crankcase. Correct location of the crankshaft without radial pressure on the ball races is imperative if premature bearing failure is to be avoided.
6 Replace the crankcase screws. The seven shorter screws are located around the main bearing housing. Tighten all the screws evenly, in a diagonal sequence.
7 Again check that the crankshaft rotates freely and that all gears can be selected.
8 Replace the nut at the rear of the crankcase mouth, but do not tighten.
9 Replace the circular steel inspection cover on the top of the crankcase. Use a new gasket and do not forget to fit the cable clip before tightening the four screws.

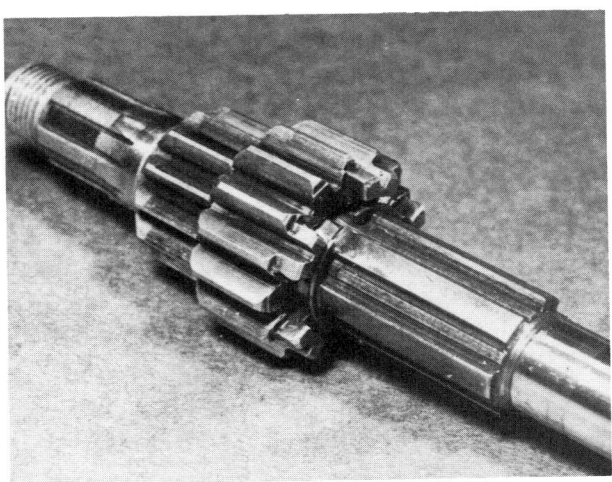

67.1 Knock over tab on oil guide lock washer

67.2 Assemble by replacing gear and circlip followed by ...

67.2a ... the sliding gear ...

67.2b ... thrust washer and ...

67.2c ... bearing and final gear

67.2d Replace the gear and circlip on the output shaft followed by ...

67.2e ... the sliding gear ...

67.2f ... thrust washer and ...

67.2g ... bearing and final gear

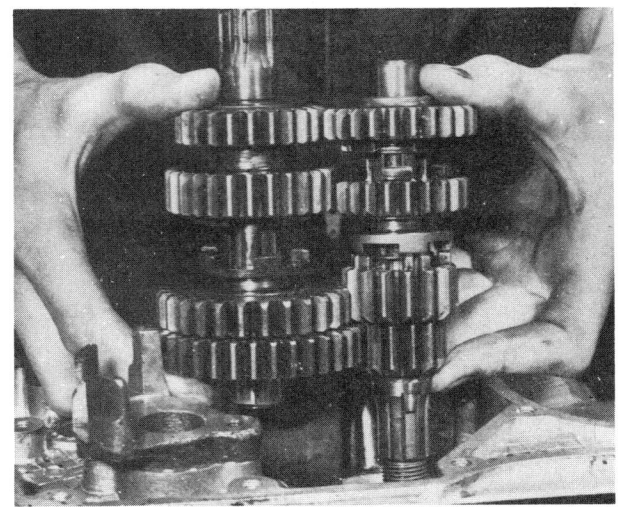

67.2h Finally, replace the assembled gears as a unit

67.3 Replace the thrust washer and ...

67.3a ... locate the selector forks

67.4 Replace the selector drum

67.5 With selector forks engaged, replace pin and thrust washer

67.6 Replace selector stop ball, spring and bolt

68.1 Assemble selector dogs in quadrant and ...

68.2 ... fit the hairpin return spring

68.3 Align dot on the quadrant with chamfered tooth

68.4 Replace the thrust washer

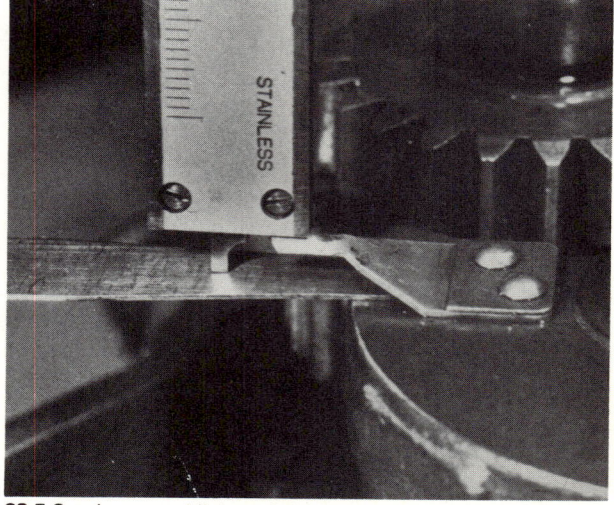

68.5 Set the neutral light switch wiper to the correct height

Chapter 1: Engine, clutch and gearbox

69.1 Replace the crankshaft assembly

69.3 Replace the right-hand crankcase

69.4 Knock in the hollow locating dowel

70 Reassembling the engine/gearbox unit - reassembling the clutch

1 Before assembling the clutch note that each major component is marked with an 'X'. When reassembling, all these marks must align.
2 Put the six clutch springs into their locations in the front clutch pressure plate and place the clutch outer drum on top.
3 Position the clutch plates on the clutch centre, starting with a faced plate. Align all the plain plate teeth and fit the whole into the clutch outer drum. Align the teeth as the plates are inserted in the drum.
4 Fit the back clutch plate and transfer the whole assembly to a vice. Gently compress the clutch in the jaws, making sure that the threaded back pressure plate pins locate in the holes of the front pressure plate.
5 When sufficient thread is protruding through the front pressure plate, replace as many of the six nuts and lockwashers as possible.
6 Remove the clutch unit from the vice and fit the remaining nuts and lockwashers. Tighten the nuts evenly and knock over the tab of the lockwashers.

69.9 Do not forget cable clip when replacing inspection cover

70.1 All balancing marks on clutch must be aligned

Chapter 1: Engine, clutch and gearbox

70.2 Replace springs in the pressure plate and ...

70.2a ... place clutch outer on top

70.3 Align clutch plate tangs and replace in clutch outer

70.4 Fit back clutch plate and ...

70.4a ... compress clutch in vice

71 Reassembling the engine/gearbox unit - replacing the primary drive and clutch

1 Gently tap the large primary gear onto its shaft. Fit a new lockwasher and replace the nut.
2 Place both the thrust washer*, chamfer downwards, and the pre-lubricated needle roller bearing over the crankshaft.
3 Remove the clutch centre and primary drive gear from the previously reassembled clutch unit - it should pull straight out. Replace the gear over the bearing on the crankshaft.
4 Replace first the thrust washer, chamfer downwards, then the spring washer.
5 Clean both the taper in the clutch unit and the taper on the crankshaft. Refit the clutch unit.
6 Temporarily replace the clutch operating mechanism and tighten the clutch nut to hold the clutch on the shaft. Lock the engine as described in Section 5 of this Chapter, to facilitate this procedure. Alternatively use a spacing tube 30 mm (1.18 in.) long.
7 With the engine still locked, tighten the nut on the large primary gear. Knock up the tab of the lockwasher.
8 Remove the castle nut and clutch operating mechanism, or spacing tube. The clutch should remain in position.

Chapter 1: Engine, clutch and gearbox

N.B. The thrust washer is available in three thicknesses; 1.9, 1.95, and 2.0 mm (0.075 in., 0.077 in. and 0.079 in.) to take up the axial play, which should be between 0.05 - 0.1 mm (0.002 - 0.004 in.). If greater than 0.1 mm (0.004 in.) noise will occur which fades when the clutch is operated. The play is difficult to measure unless a dial test indicator is available. If excessive play is suspected the engine will have to be returned to an MZ agent for measurement. To use a dial test indicator, replace the thrust washer, needle roller bearing, primary drive gear and upper thrust washer. Make a spacer that will clamp the thrust washer in position, when the castellated nut is tightened. Clamp the dial test indicator so that it contacts the top of the primary gear and measure the axial clearance. Fit the appropriate thrust washer to take up the axial play, leaving only the small amount specified.

72 Reassembling the engine/gearbox unit - replacing the kickstart, left-hand engine cover and clutch operating mechanism

1 Renew both the kickstart and gear lever shaft rubber 'O' rings in the left-hand engine cover.
2 Assemble the kickstart shaft and mechanism.
3 Replace the kickstart mechanism into the cover locating the tang of the return spring in the lug. Do not forget the thrust washer.
4 Place the end of the shaft in a vice fitted with soft jaws. Rotate the cover through approximately 1¼ turns anti-clockwise and replace the cotter pin. Tighten the cotter pin nut.
5 Replace the clutch operating worm and bearing in the cover. Set the operating arm so that it is approximately 6 mm from the centre of the nipple to the cover lug, with the worm fully home and touching the bearing housing.
6 Replace the distance collar on the end of the crankshaft.
7 Fit a new gasket and replace the cover making sure that the clip on the kickstart mechanism engages in the crankcase. TS250 models differ slightly, being fitted with a slotted operating cam instead of a clip. The cam must locate in the crankcase with the slot downwards over the cover retaining screw hole.
8 Replace the five screws complete with copper washers and tighten them evenly in a diagonal sequence.
9 Tighten down the castellated nut to a torque wrench setting of 65 lb ft and replace the split pin.
10 Replace the adjuster plate, fit a new rubber 'O' ring and replace the adjuster plate cover. Tighten the three screws. The slotted holes in the adjuster plate enable the coarse adjustment of the clutch to be made if, due to wear, the handlebar lever adjuster is unable to cope.

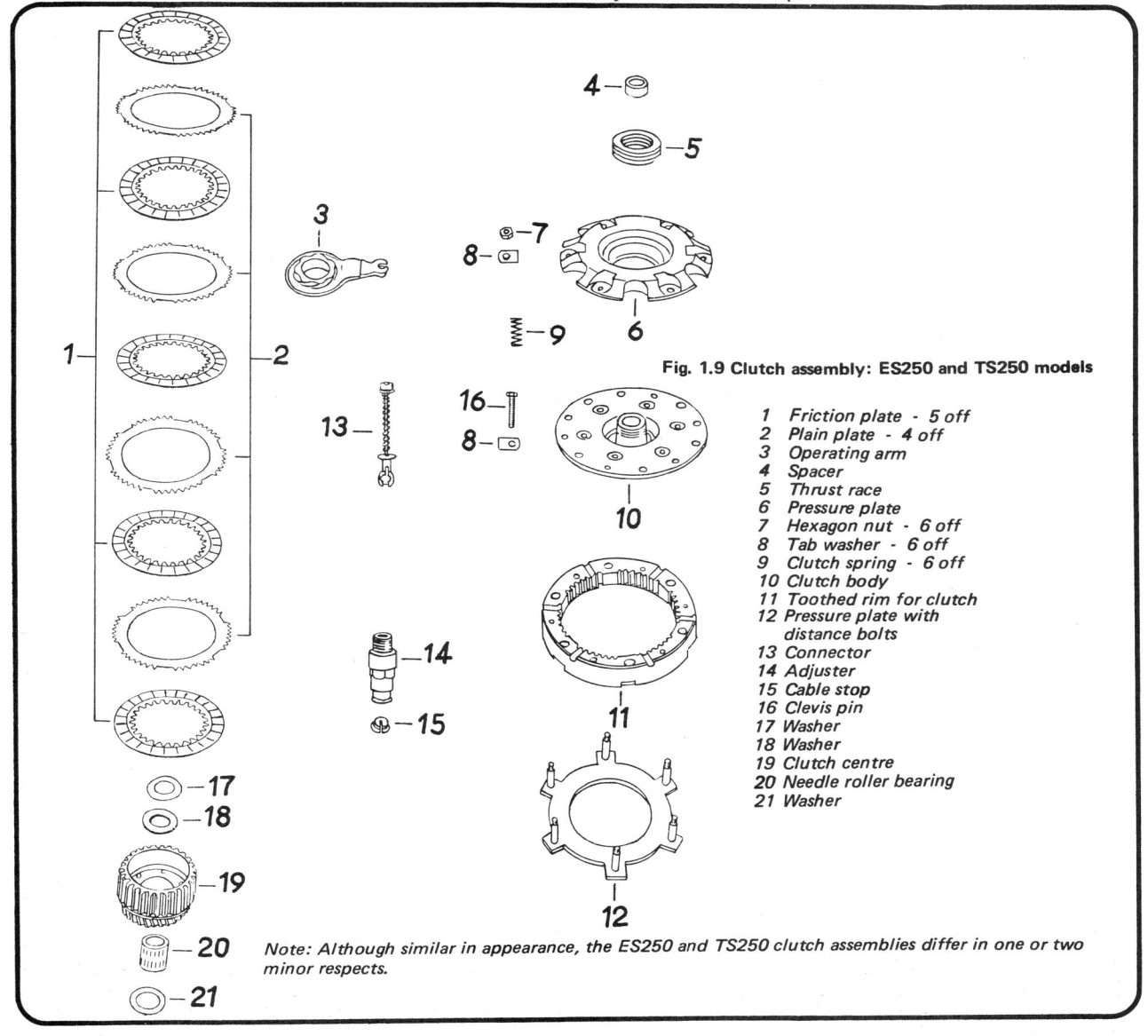

Fig. 1.9 Clutch assembly: ES250 and TS250 models

1 Friction plate - 5 off
2 Plain plate - 4 off
3 Operating arm
4 Spacer
5 Thrust race
6 Pressure plate
7 Hexagon nut - 6 off
8 Tab washer - 6 off
9 Clutch spring - 6 off
10 Clutch body
11 Toothed rim for clutch
12 Pressure plate with distance bolts
13 Connector
14 Adjuster
15 Cable stop
16 Clevis pin
17 Washer
18 Washer
19 Clutch centre
20 Needle roller bearing
21 Washer

Note: Although similar in appearance, the ES250 and TS250 clutch assemblies differ in one or two minor respects.

71.1 Replace the primary drive gear and ...

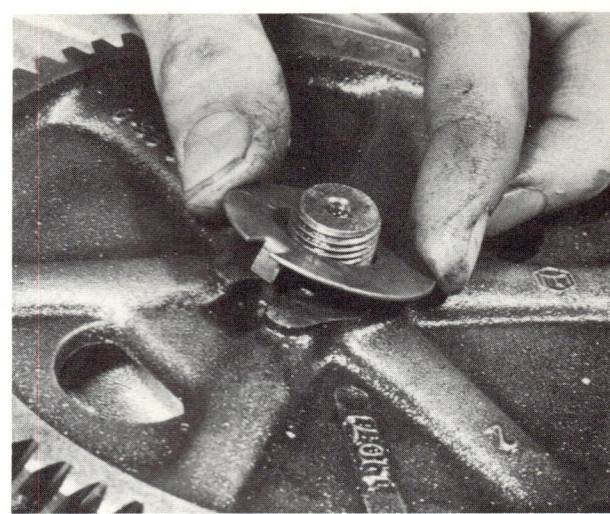

71.1a ... lockwasher

71.2 Replace thrust washer, chamfer downwards, and bearing

71.3 Slide on clutch centre

71.4 Replace thrust washer, chamfer downwards and belled spring washer

71.5 Clean tapers and replace the clutch unit

71.6 Temporarily fit clutch operating worm for clutch to be tightened

71.7 Knock up the tab on the lockwasher

72.1 Renew the rubber O-ring oil seals

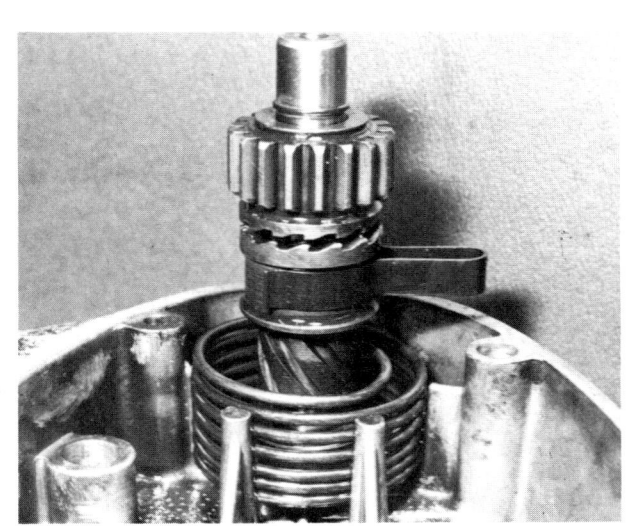

72.3 Replace the kickstart mechanism

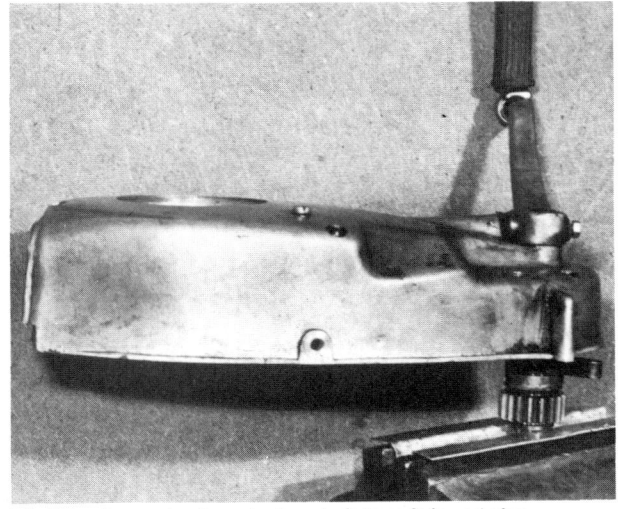

72.4 Tension spring by gripping shaft in soft jawed vice ...

72.4a ... replace the cotter pin

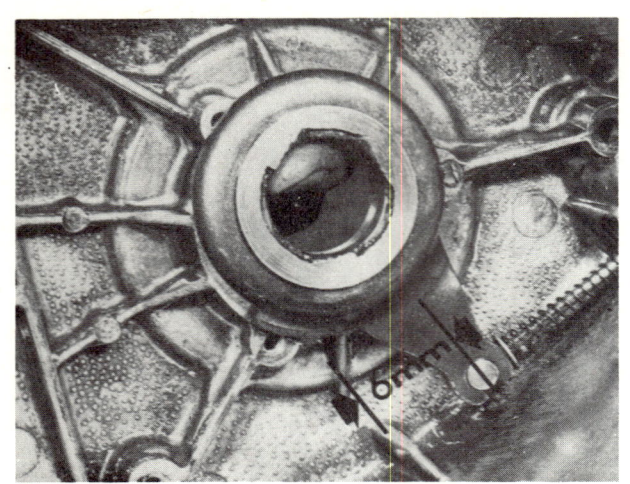

Chapter 1: Engine, clutch and gearbox

72.5 Set clutch operating worm as shown

72.7 Replace left-hand cover. Position the kickstart clip ...

72.7a ... so that it engages in the crankcase

72.9 Tighten castellated nut and replace split pin

72.10 Replace the clutch adjuster cover

73 Reassembling the engine/gearbox unit - replacing and shimming the oil seal cups

1 Replace the sealing cups on both the gearbox mainshaft and crankshaft. Use new gaskets and oil seals. Do not forget the shims, where fitted, and fit the crankshaft cup with the outer oil channels at the top and bottom. Tighten the screws evenly and in a diagonal sequence.
N.B. If the main bearings have been disturbed, or a new crankshaft fitted, it will be necessary to re-shim the cups to maintain the correct clearance. Measure the following with a vernier caliper:

A Distance the bearing protrudes from the crankcase ie; machined face of crankcase to top of bearing outer ring.
B Distance between gasket face and shim face of the sealing cup.
C Gasket thickness

All measurements in mm
The shim thickness, S, can then be calculated using the following formula:

For crankshaft $S = (B + C) - (A + 0.2 \text{ to } 0.3)$
For gearbox $S = (A + D) - (B + 0.3 \text{ to } 0.4)$

Chapter 1: Engine, clutch and gearbox   49

73.1 Do not omit shims when replacing gearbox oil seal cup and ...

73.1a ... crankshaft oil seal cup

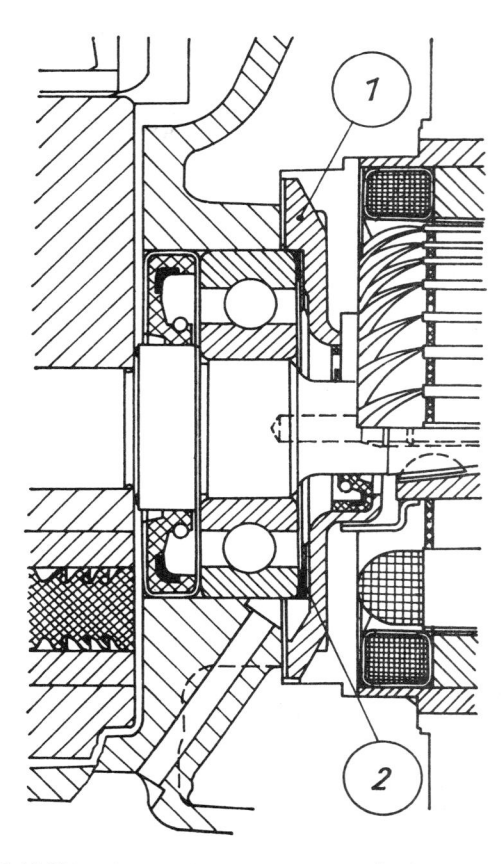

Fig. 1.10 Shimming the dynamo oil seal cup (250 cc models)

1 Radial sealing ring of bearing cup
2 Shim(s)

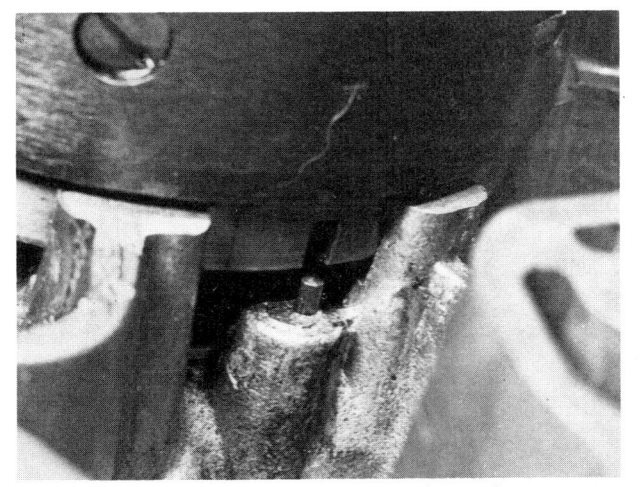

74.2 Slot in dynamo outer locates over crankcase pin

74 Reassembling the engine/gearbox unit - replacing the dynamo

1 Fit the roller key to the crankshaft. Clean the taper and replace the dynamo armature and contact breaker cam. Make sure that the slot in the contact breaker cam locates on the peg of the armarure. Replace the armature bolt and tighten.
2 Replace the dynamo outer. Make sure that the slot aligns with the peg in the crankcase. Replace and tighten the two retaining screws.
3 Replace the two carbon brushes.
4 See Chapter 3 for the procedure used to time the ignition and adjust the contact breaker.

75 Reassembling the engine/gearbox unit - replacing the gearbox sprocket

1 Reconnect the neutral indicator light switch lead.
2 Replace the gearbox sprocket, lockwasher and nut.
3 Tighten the nut. Either lock the engine as described in Section 5 of this Chapter after placing it in gear, or use the rear chain to jam the sprocket. Do not forget to bend up the tab on the lockwasher.

Chapter 1: Engine, clutch and gearbox

76 Reassembling the engine/gearbox unit - replacing the piston, cylinder barrel and head

1 Replace the piston rings on the piston after having checked their end gaps, see Specification. Locate each ring gap over the peg in the piston groove.
2 Replace one of the piston circlips. Always use new circlips. Make sure that the circlip is seated in its groove correctly.
3 Oil and replace the small-end bearing.
4 If the gudgeon pin is a tight fit in the piston, pre-heat the piston in some hot water to facilitate refitting the pin.
5 Place the piston over the connecting rod the correct way round, with the arrow pointing forwards towards the exhaust port. Insert the gudgeon pin. Replace the other piston circlip, making sure it is seated properly.
6 Fit a new cylinder base gasket. Make sure that the gasket does not protrude into the transfer ports. Cut to shape with scissors, if necessary.
7 Oil the piston rings and check that they are still correctly positioned. Remove any rag that may have been placed in the crankcase mouth.
8 Slide the cylinder barrel down the studs over the piston and rings whilst compressing the latter with your fingers. Push the barrel right home. If it is tight, loosen the nut at the rear of the crankcase mouth. Do not forget to retighten the nut screws afterwards.
9 If the engine has an inclined spark plug and has to be retimed, do not fit the cylinder head yet. It will be necessary to set the ignition timing as described in Chapter 3.
10 Check the head and barrel joint faces are clean and fit a new gasket. Do not use jointing compound.
11 Tighten down the cylinder head nuts diagonally to a torque wrench setting of 21 lbf ft (250 models) or 15 lbf ft (150 models).

77 Reassembling the engine/gearbox unit - refitting the engine in the frame

1 Engine replacement is a reversal of Section 43 of this Chapter.
2 For sppedometer drive gearbox reassembly (ES250 models) see Chapter 5, Section 14.4.
3 Do not forget to refill the gearbox/clutch with the correct quantity of oil.

78 Starting and running the rebuilt engine

Refer to Section 37 of this Chapter.

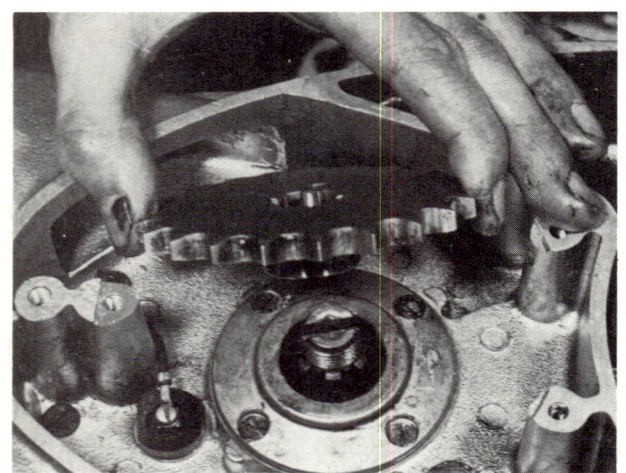

75.2 Replace the gearbox sprocket

76.1 Fit piston rings as shown

76.3 Oil and replace the small end bearing

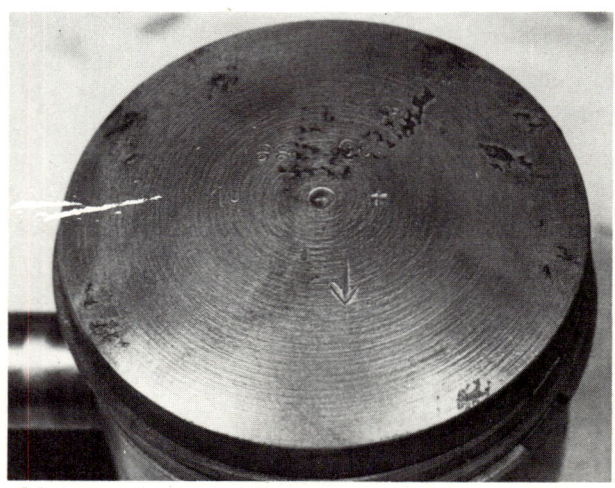

76.5 Arrow on piston must point forwards

76.5a Push in the gudgeon pin and ...

76.5b Fit new circlips

76.8 Slide the barrel over the studs

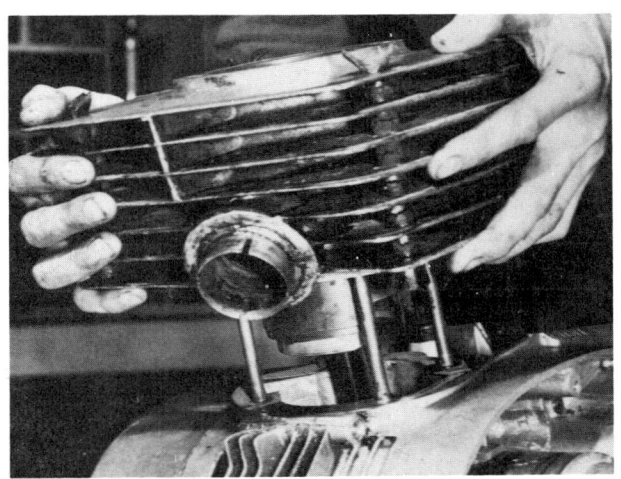

76.10 Use a new gasket when replacing cylinder head

Chapter 1: Engine, clutch and gearbox

79 Fault diagnosis - engine

Symptom	Cause	Remedy
Engine will not start	Defective spark plug	Remove the plug and lay it on the cylinder head. Check whether a good spark occurs when ignition is switched on and engine is rotated.
	Dirty or closed contact breaker points	Check condition of points and whether gap is correct.
	Faulty or disconnected condenser	Check whether points arc when separated. Replace condenser if evidence of arcing or if a weak spark is obtained and the plug is in good condition.
Engine runs unevenly	Ignition and/or fuel system fault	Check each system independantly as though engine will not start.
	Blowing cylinder head gasket	Leak should be evident from oil leakage where gas escapes.
	Incorrect ignition timing	Check accuracy and if necessary reset.
	Damaged oil seals	Check crankcase oil seals and renew as necessary.
Lack of power	Fault in fuel system or incorrect ignition timing	See above.
Excessive mechanical noise	Worn cylinder barrel (piston slap)	Rebore and fit oversize piston.
	Worn big-end bearings (knock)	Fit replacement crankshaft assembly.
	Worn main bearings (rumble)	Fit new journal bearings and oil seals.

80 Fault diagnosis - gearbox

Symptom	Cause	Remedy
Difficulty in engaging gears	Selector forks bent	Replace.
	Gear clusters not assembled correctly	Check gear cluster arrangement and position of thrust washers.
Machine jumps out of gear	Worn dogs on ends of gear pinions	Replace worn pinions.
Gearchange lever does not return to original position	Broken return spring	Replace spring.
Kickstarter does not return when engine is turned over or started	Broken or poorly tensioned return spring	Replace spring or retension.
Kickstarter slips	Ratchet assembly worn	Renew all worn parts.

81 Fault diagnosis - clutch

Symptom	Cause	Remedy
Engine speed increases out of proportion to road speed	Clutch slip	Check clutch adjustment for free play at handlebar lever. Check thickness of lined plates.
Difficulty in engaging gears. Gear changes jerky and machine creeps forward when clutch is withdrawn. Difficulty in selecting neutral	Clutch drag	Check clutch adjustment for too much free play. Check clutch drums for indentations in slots and clutch plates for burrs on tongues. Dress with file if damage not too great.
Clutch operation stiff	Damaged, trapped or frayed control cable	Check cable and replace if necessary. Make sure cable is lubricated and has no sharp bends.
	Bent operating pushrod	Check the pushrod for trueness.

Chapter 2 Fuel system and lubrication

Contents

General description ... 1	Carburettor - float level ... 7
Petrol/oil mix - correct ratio ... 2	Carburettor - adjusting tickover and jet settings ... 8
Petrol tank - removal and replacement ... 3	Air cleaner - location, examination and replacement ... 9
Petrol tap - removal, renovation and replacement ... 4	Exhaust system - cleaning ... 10
Carburettor - removal and replacement ... 5	Engine/gearbox lubrication ... 11
Carburettor - dismantling, examination and reassembly ... 6	Fault diagnosis - fuel system, carburation and lubrication ... 12

Specifications

Carburettor	ES150, TS150*	ES250, TS250*
Type	BVF 24N1-1	BVF 28N1-1
Choke size - mm	24	28
Main jet	92 (95)	107 (115)
Needle jet	65	67
Needle	C3	K3 5 grooves (C5 5 grooves)
Needle position:		
Grooves from top	3 or 4	3 or 4
Running in	4	4
Starting jet	75	100
Pilot jet	— (40)	40
Float needle valve	—	18
Pilot setting:		
Turns out	2½ (2-3)	2-3
Throttle slide cutaway	3 (—)	—

Figures in brackets refer to TS models, where different from ES models.

Gearbox/clutch oil capacity - cc ...	450	750

1 General description

The fuel is gravity fed to a BVF carburettor which is fitted with a cold start device. The petroil is filtered by a gauze in the petrol tap, which is also fitted with a sediment bowl. The air to the carburettor passes through a paper element.

Engine lubrication is by petrol/oil mixture. The gearbox and clutch are separately lubricated by their own oil supply.

2 Petrol/oil mix - correct ratio

1 Because the engine relies on the 'petroil' system for lubrication purposes, a measured amount of oil must always be added to the petrol. The correct mixing ratio is TS250 50 : 1, all other models 33 : 1.
2 It will be realised that the lubrication of the engine is dependent solely on the intake of the fuel mixture from the carburettor. In consequence it is inadvisable to coast the machine down a long hill whilst the throttle is closed otherwise there is risk of engine seizure through the temporary lack of lubrication.
3 On no account use the same mixture for the gearbox, which has its own separate oil content, shared with the clutch assembly.

3 Petrol tank - removal and replacement

1 Turn off the petrol tap and disconnect the fuel pipe.

ES models
2 Remove the two securing screws from the handlebar cover plate. Undo and remove the two bolts underneath the rear of the tank. Note the anti-vibration rubber bushes. Lift up the seat on the hinge. Lift and pull off the petrol tank from the rear.

Chapter 2: Fuel system and lubrication

TS models

3 Undo and remove the through bolt at the rear of the petrol tank. Lift and pull off the petrol tank from the rear.
4 Replace the tank by reversing the above procedure. Before replacing the tank, check the condition of the anti-vibration rubbers. Renew as necessary. On no account omit the rubbers or rigidly mount the tank because of the risk of it splitting from vibration.

4 Petrol tap - removal, renovation and replacement

1 Disconnect the petrol pipe and drain the tank.
2 The tap is removed by undoing the top union nut.
3 Unscrew the sediment bowl and clean it out with a little petrol. If the tap has been leaking, remove the two screws and lift out the retaining plate and tap lever. This exposes a rubber seal which is probably the cause of the leakage. Renew the seal and reassemble the tap.
4 Replace the tap by reversing the above procedure. Before reconnecting the petrol pipe, check that the plastic has not become hard and brittle. Renew it if necessary.

5 Carburettor - removal and replacement

1 Turn off the petrol tap and remove the petrol pipe from either the tap or carburettor.
2 Lift off the carburettor shield (ES models only), after removing the central retaining screw.
3 Pull off the rubber induction hose from the carburettor, after slackening the hose clip (where fitted).
4 Pull up the rubber protecting cap and unscrew the carburettor top ring nut. Carefully pull out the throttle slide and needle. Remove the throttle cable by pushing it in and to one side.
5 Unscrew the cold start device. If required, the plunger can be removed first by releasing the cable tension at the choke lever and then turning and sliding the cable nipple out from the plunger.
6 The carburettor can either be removed by itself or complete with the inlet manifold. To remove the carburettor only, slacken the pinch bolt and pull the carburettor away from the manifold. To remove the manifold complete with carburettor, undo the two bolts (150 models) or two nuts (250 models) at the cylinder barrel. Note the arrangement of the gaskets and heat insulator.
7 Replace the carburettor by reversing the dismantling procedure. Fit new gaskets where appropriate. Make sure the carburettor is in a vertical position and not canted to one side, when reinstalled.

4.2 Undo union nut to remove tap

5.4 Needle is held in position by return spring

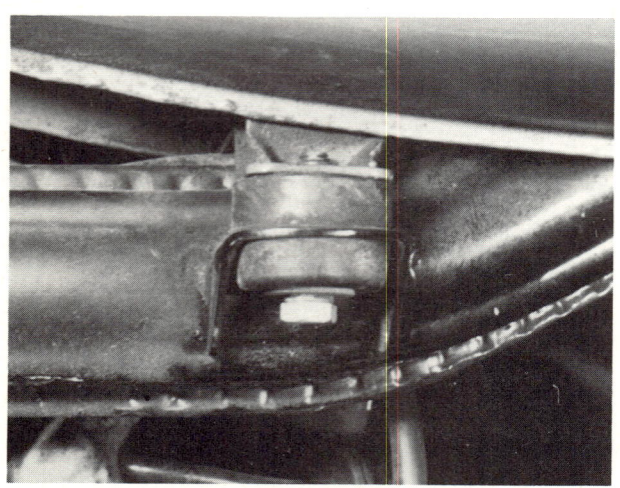

3.2 Anti vibration rubbers are fitted to tank

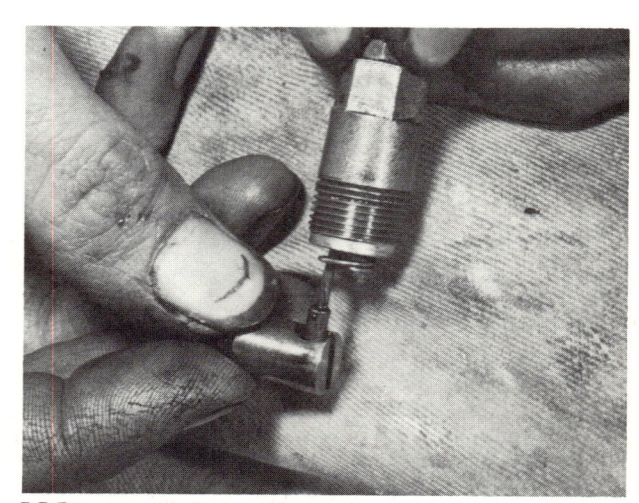

5.5 Remove cable from cold start plunger

Fig. 2.1 BVF 30 N2-3 carburettor cross section

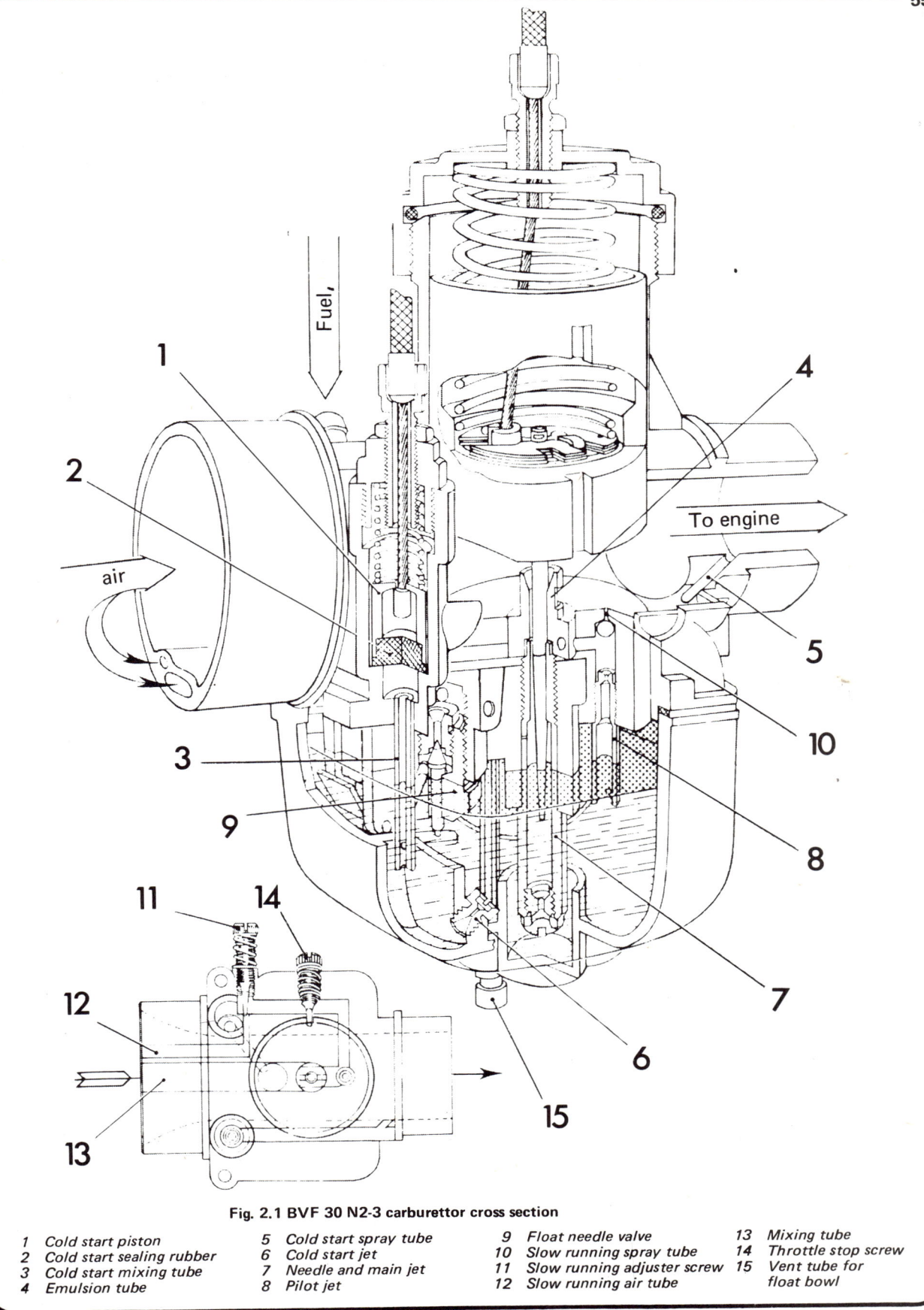

1 Cold start piston
2 Cold start sealing rubber
3 Cold start mixing tube
4 Emulsion tube
5 Cold start spray tube
6 Cold start jet
7 Needle and main jet
8 Pilot jet
9 Float needle valve
10 Slow running spray tube
11 Slow running adjuster screw
12 Slow running air tube
13 Mixing tube
14 Throttle stop screw
15 Vent tube for float bowl

6 Carburettor - dismantling, examination and reassembly

1 The same basic carburettor is fitted to all models, the difference being the choke sizes and jets, see Specifications. The only exception occurs in the case of the TS250 model which is fitted with a throttle stop screw to adjust the idling speed, instead of using the throttle cable. The stripdown procedure, however, remains the same.
2 Remove the carburettor, throttle slide and cold start device as described in the previous Section.
3 Access to all the jets and the float is obtained by removing the three screws retaining the float bowl and lifting the float bowl off.
4 The dual float is removed by gently drifting out its pivot pin with a pin punch.
5 The main jet assembly should be removed with a socket or ring spanner to avoid damage. When removing the pilot jet be careful not to damage it with the screwdriver.
6 The cold start device jet is located in the bottom of the float bowl and can be removed with a screwdriver, if desired.
7 The float needle assembly should also be removed, using a socket or ring spanner. Use the spanner to hold the assembly when unscrewing the float needle seat from the main body.
8 If required, the throttle slide guide and emulsion tube can be removed by undoing the two screws in the base of the main body. Before removal, note the position of the emulsion tube since it is asymmetrical.
9 The slow running mixture screw and throttle stop screw (where fitted) are removed by unscrewing them. Note their original positions.
10 With the carburettor dismantled, check the throttle needle for straightness by rolling it on a flat surface; also check it is not worn where it slides in the needle jet. If worn, renew both the needle and jet.
11 Check the throttle slide for excessive wear. Renew as necessary.
12 Inspect the float needle and seat. Renew the pair if either appears to be damaged.
13 Check the float for leakage. The easiest way is by shaking it; if liquid can be heard inside it is leaking and should be renewed.
14 Check the condition of the rubber sealing disc in the cold start device plunger. Renew if necessary.
15 Check that the taper on the slow running screw is not scored. Renew if necessary.
16 Reassemble in the reverse order, making sure that the needle clip is located in the correct needle groove. Make sure the emulsion tube is the correct way round, with the smaller vertical bar facing towards the engine. When replacing the jets **do not overtighten them**.
17 When replacing the slow running adjustment screw, screw it right home but **do not use force**, then back it off the correct amount, see Specifications. Always use new gaskets.
18 For float level settings see the following Section.

7 Carburettor - float level

1 Check the closing of the float needle valve as shown in Fig. 2.2A. Adjust the height by bending the operating lever A.
2 The opening of the float needle should also be checked as shown in Fig. 2.2B. Adjust the distance by bending the top lever B. (See page 60).
N.B. Use the correct fibre washers ie; 1.5 mm thick, otherwise the desired levels will not be obtained. Also check that both floats are the same height.

8 Carburettor - adjusting tickover and jet settings

1 When adjusting the tickover the engine must be at its normal working temperature and the machine should be standing on level ground.

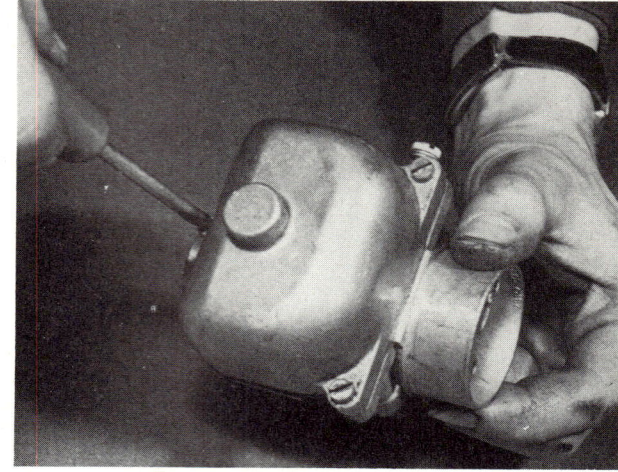

6.3 The float chamber is held by three screws

6.4 Remove the float pivot pin

6.5 Unscrew the main jet assembly followed by ...

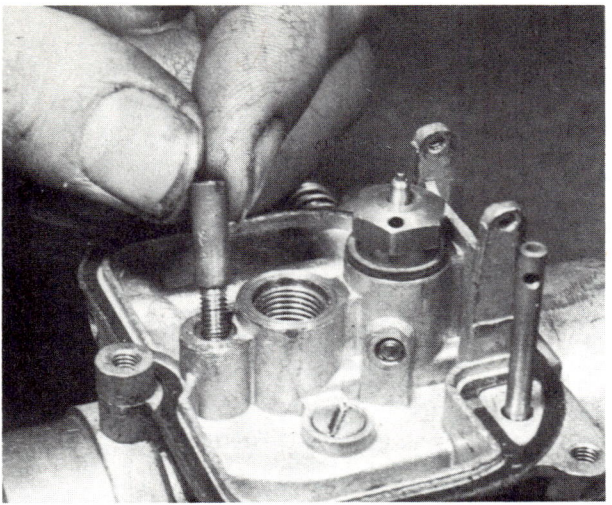

6.5a ... the pilot jet

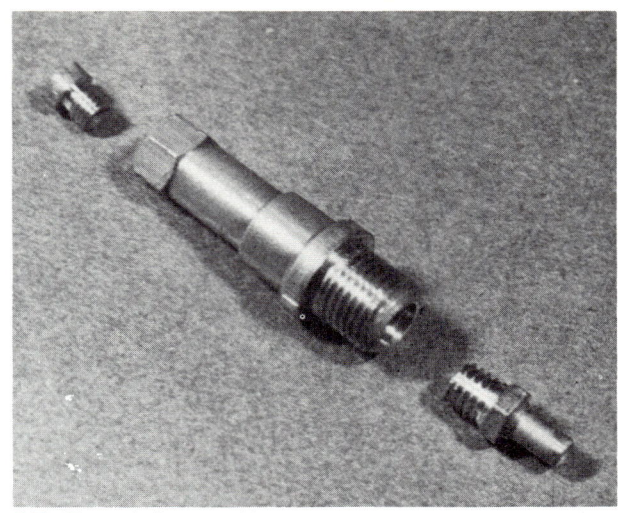

6.5b The main jet assembly

6.6 Cold start jet can be found in float bowl

6.7 Remove the float needle assembly

6.7a The float needle assembly

6.8 Remove the two screws and ...

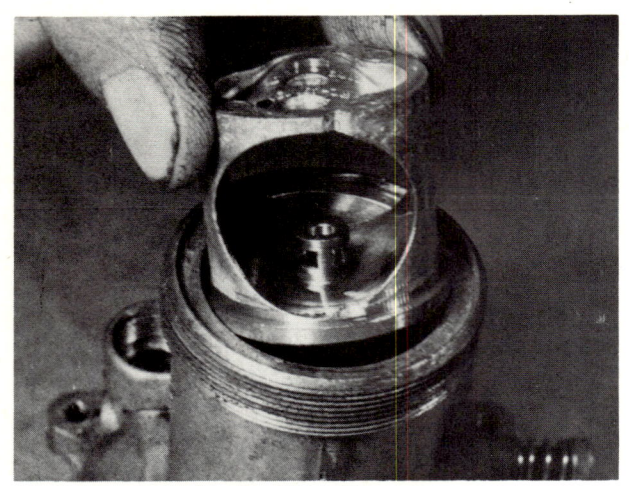

Chapter 2: Fuel system and lubrication

6.8a ... lift out the throttle slide guide

6.16 Position needle clip in the correct groove

6.16a The emulsion tube viewed from the rear and ...

6.16b ... the front (engine side)

2 Initially, the carburettor should be set as per the Specifications.
3 With the engine running, adjust the cable* or throttle stop screw (whichever is applicable) to obtain a fast tickover speed.
4 Screw the slow running mixture screw either in or out until the engine runs evenly without hunting or misfiring. If necessary, reduce the engine speed by readjusting the cable or throttle stop screw. Readjust the mixture screw as necessary. Do not set the engine tickover too slow otherwise there is a risk that the engine may stall when the throttle is closed during normal running, especially when it is cold.
5 The sizes of the jets and needle are set by the manufacturer and under normal circumstances should not require any alteration. They have been selected after exhaustive testing.
6 If it is considered an alteration is required, firstly check that the correct jets have been fitted (see Specifications). Then check the engine for other faults which can give similar indications eg; a weak mixture resulting from an air leak in the carburettor manifold or filter system.
7 When making any adjustments it is best to err slightly on the rich side, since too weak a mixture can cause extensive damage through overheating.
*N.B. The twistgrip is spring loaded and if twisted past the tickover position will lower the throttle slide right down and thereby stop the engine. When adjusting the tickover speed, the twistgrip should not be touched and should be in the normal tickover position.

9 Air cleaner - location, examination and replacement

1 The air cleaner is located behind the left-hand side cover on all 150 models; in the right-hand side cover of the ES250 models and in the left-hand side cover of the TS250 model.
2 Clean the element by tapping it lightly to loosen the dust, then use a soft brush to dust the outer surfaces of the element. If compressed air is available, blow gently from **inside** the element.
3 If the filter has become oily it will have to be renewed. It should also be renewed if there are any holes or damage to the corrugated element.
4 On no account should the machine be used without a filter since this will weaken the mixture and cause damage by overheating. The carburettor is jetted to take into account the air flow restriction of the air cleaner element.
5 When replacing the air filter make sure that all the sealing washers are in good condition, otherwise a weak mixture will result, caused by leaks.

Chapter 2: Fuel system and lubrication 59

10 Exhaust system - cleaning

1 The exhaust system of a two-stroke is highly susceptible to blockage due to the burning of the oil in the two-stroke mixture. It is imperative to keep the exhaust system clear or the carbon will build up and cause excessive back pressure with the consequent loss of performance and efficiency.

2 On some models it is possible to partially strip the silencer by removing the two nuts in the centre of the exhaust tail piece and pulling off the tail piece from the silencer main body. Remove as much carbon as possible with a wire brush.

3 The only way to satisfactorily clean the inside of the silencer is by dissolving the oil etc. with a solution of caustic soda. The solution is prepared by adding approximately 3 lbs of caustic soda to a gallon of cold water, whilst stirring. Add the caustic soda a little at a time since a considerable amount of heat is evolved. Be extremely careful with this solution since it is highly corrosive and can cause serious burns. Wear protective clothing and safety glasses. Wash out the exhaust system thoroughly afterwards, using plenty of water.

Warning: On no account use caustic soda on aluminium, aluminium alloy or magnesium components, since it will attack and dissolve them.

4 If necessary, the silencer can be left overnight with the solution inside, provided it has been removed from the machine and has a tight fitting bung in one end.

11 Engine/gearbox - lubrication

1 The engine is lubricated by the petroil mixture from the fuel tank and does not require separate lubrication.

2 The gearbox and clutch share a separate oil content which should be changed periodically (see Routine maintenance). It is best to drain the oil when it is hot ie; after the engine has been running for some time.

3 Firstly remove the filler plug. On the 150 cc models there are two drain plugs, both on the left-hand side, one underneath the gearbox and the other underneath the left-hand engine cover. The 250 cc models have only one drain plug which is underneath the right-hand side of the gearbox in an inclined position. Do not remove the central bolt since this is part of the gear selector mechanism.

4 Refill the gearbox with the correct quantity of oil after replacing the drain plug. Do not use graphited oil or molybdenium disulphide additives since they will promote clutch slip.

5 To check the oil level remove the oil level screw and allow the excess oil to run out. On the 150 cc models the screw is located below the kickstart/gear lever shafts. On 250 cc models it is below and to the right of the circular clutch adjustment cover plate.

9.1 The air filter is behind the left-hand side cover (TS150) or ...

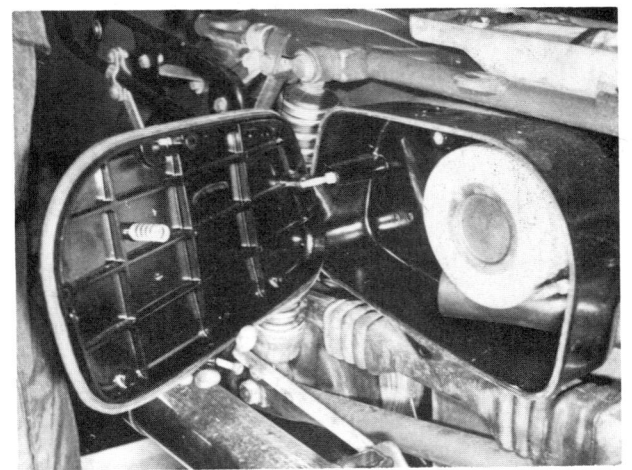

9.1a ... in the right-hand side cover (ES250)

10.2 Remove the tailpiece nuts and tailpiece to expose the ...

10.2a ...silencer main body

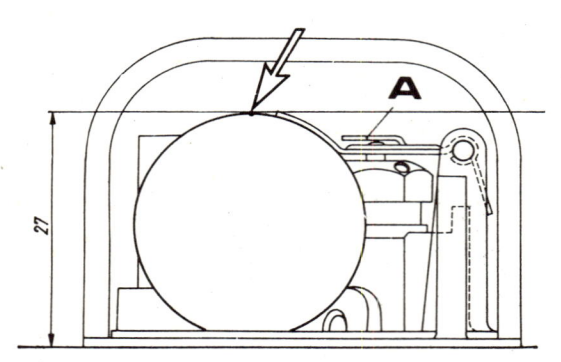

Fig. 2.2a Float level adjustment: closed float valve

A Float needle valve lever

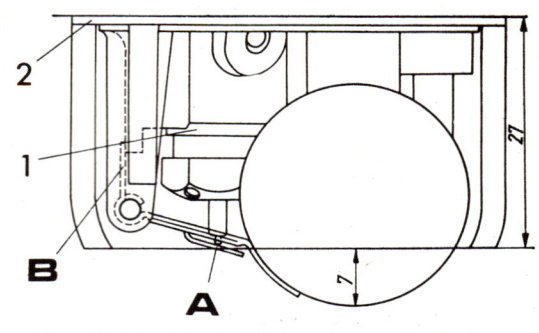

Fig. 2.2b Float level adjustment: open float valve

A Float needle valve lever
B Stop lever
1 Washer 1.5 mm thick
2 Washer 0.5 mm thick

12 Fault diagnosis - fuel system and lubrication

Symptom	Cause	Remedy
Excessive fuel consumption	Air cleaner choked or restricted	Clean or if paper element fitted, renew.
	Fuel leaking from carburettor. Float sticking	Check all unions and gaskets. Float needle seat needs cleaning.
	Badly worn or distorted carburettor	Replace.
	Carburettor incorrectly adjusted	Tune and adjust as necessary.
	Incorrect silencer fitted to exhaust system	Do not deviate from manufacturer's original silencer design.
Idling speed too high	Throttle stop screw in too far. Carburettor top loose	Adjust screw. Tighten top.
Engine does not respond to throttle	Back pressure in silencer. Float displaced or punctured	Check baffles in silencer. Check whether float is correctly located or has petrol inside.
	Use of incorrect silencer or baffles missing	See above. Do not run without baffles.
Engine dies after running for a short while	Blocked air hole in filler cap	Clean.
Engine lacks response and overheats	Weak mixture	Check for partial blockage in carburettor.
	Air cleaner disconnected	Reconnect. Check hoses for splits.
	Modified silencer has upset carburation	Replace with original.
	Air leak at carburettor joint or in crankcase	Check joints to eliminate leakage.
Engine spits back into carburettor	Weak mixture	Check and adjust carburettor settings, also check for air leaks.
Engine loses power under load	Lubrication failure	Stop engine immediately and check petroil ratio.
Excessive white smoke from exhaust	Too much oil in petrol, or oil has separated out	Mix in recommended ratio only. Mix thoroughly if mixing pump not available.

Chapter 3 Ignition system

Contents

General description ... 1	Contact breakers - removal, examination and replacement ... 5
Ignition coil - function and checking ... 2	Contact breaker - adjustment ... 6
Condenser - function, removal and replacement ... 3	Ignition timing ... 7
Automatic ignition advance unit - removal, examination and replacement ... 4	Spark plugs - checking and resetting the gaps ... 8
	Fault diagnosis - ignition system ... 9

Specifications

	ES150	TS150	ES250, TS250
Ignition timing BTDC - mm	4.0 (0.16 in.)	3.0-3.5 (0.12 - 0.14 in.)	3.0* (0.12 in.)

*Setting with bobweights fully expanded, equivalent to 22° 15' crank angle.

Contact breaker gap - mm	0.4 (0.016 in.)	0.3 - 0.4 (0.012 - 0.016 in.)	0.3 (0.012 in.)
Spark plug gap - mm ...	0.5 (0.020 in.)	0.5 (0.020 in.)	0.5 (0.020 in.)

1 General description

The MZs are fitted with a 6 volt negative earth conventional contact breaker/coil ignition system. An emergency ignition position on the ignition switch, is provided for use when the battery is discharged. This position allows the output from the dynamo to go directly to the ignition coil.

Opening and closing of the contact breaker every revolution, causes a magnetic field in the primary winding of the ignition coil to build up and then collapse. This induces a high voltage in the secondary windings which causes the spark to occur across the electrodes of the spark plug.

2 Ignition coil - function and checking

1 The ignition coil consists of primary and secondary windings mounted on a soft iron core. It operates in conjunction with the contact breaker to convert low voltage from the battery into the high voltage necessary for the spark.

2 The ignition coil is a sealed unit designed to give long service, without the need for attention. It is located above the battery, under the left-hand side cover. If a weak spark and difficult starting causes the performance of the coil to be suspect it should be tested by an MZ agent or an auto-electrical expert, who will have the appropriate test equipment. A faulty coil must be replaced; it is not possible to effect a satisfactory repair.

3 A defective condenser can give the illusion of a faulty coil and for this reason it is advisable to investigate the condition of the condenser before condemning the ignition coil. Also check that the battery is charged and functioning correctly.

3 Condenser - function, removal and replacement

1 The condenser has two functions. Firstly it reduces sparking at the contacts (and hence prevents rapid wear of the points). Its second and most important function is to greatly increase the induced voltage in the secondary windings of the coil and hence the strength of the high tension spark at break. In practice, without the condenser the spark is very weak, and the bike will not run smoothly.

2 The condenser is located close to the contact breaker and is held by a strap retained by a screw. Before removing the condenser, detach the connecting link to the contact breaker by undoing the screw in the top of the condenser.

3 If the condenser malfunctions, no repair can be undertaken and a replacement will have to be obtained. If malfunction is suspected, fit a new condenser in place of the original and observe the effect on engine performance. If the fault persists, most probably the ignition coil is at fault.

4 Automatic ignition advance unit - removal, examination and replacement

1 The early 250 cc models are fitted with an automatic advance mechanism. This mechanism is located behind the contact breaker operating cam and should give little trouble.

2 To remove the mechanism, undo and remove the dynamo armature retaining bolt which allows the unit to be pulled clear.

3 If the unit is stiff or seized, strip it down by removing the two split pins and washers and by pulling the cam off its pivot. Clean and regrease, using either a graphited or molybdenum

Chapter 3: Ignition system

based grease. Check the condition of the two springs. Renew them, if necessary.
4 Reassemble and replace the unit by reversing the above procedure.

5 Contact breaker - removal, examination and replacement

1 Remove the right-hand engine cover, which exposes the contact breaker mounted on the dynamo outer.
2 To remove the contact breaker, undo the nut and lift off the connecting link to the condenser. Undo and remove the lower contact breaker screw which frees the contact breaker assembly.
3 Check the contact breaker points for pitting and/or burning. If this is only slight it can be removed with a small oil stone or emery. Be careful to keep the contact faces square. If wear is severe renew the contact breaker points assembly.
4 When reassembling, lightly grease the contact breaker pin with a graphited or molybdenum grease. Do not forget to replace the insulating washers.
5 Soak the lubricating felt pads in a hypoid oil and squeeze out the excess before refitting. The felts should be adjusted so that they just touch the lobe of the cam.
6 Refit the contact breaker by reversing the dismantling procedure. Readjustment of the points gap will be necessary after attention. See the following Section.

5.2 Undo nut to remove contact breaker points assembly

3.2 Detach the connecting link before removing condenser

5.5 Lubricate both felt pads

5.1 The contact breaker assembly

6 Contact breaker - adjustment

1 After checking the condition of the contact breaker (see previous Section), turn the crankshaft until the high lobe of the cam contacts the heel of the contact breaker, and the points are open to their fullest extent.
2 Slacken the bottom contact breaker screw and adjust the gap by turning the higher screw in the appropriate direction. Once the gap has been correctly set using a feeler gauge (see Specifications) tighten the lower screw. Check the gap again and readjust if necessary.
3 The contact breaker gap must be within the prescribed limits if optimum performance is to be achieved. If the gap is too small it will retard the ignition setting and if too large, the ignition will be over-advanced.

6.2 Set the contact breaker cam to give the widest opening

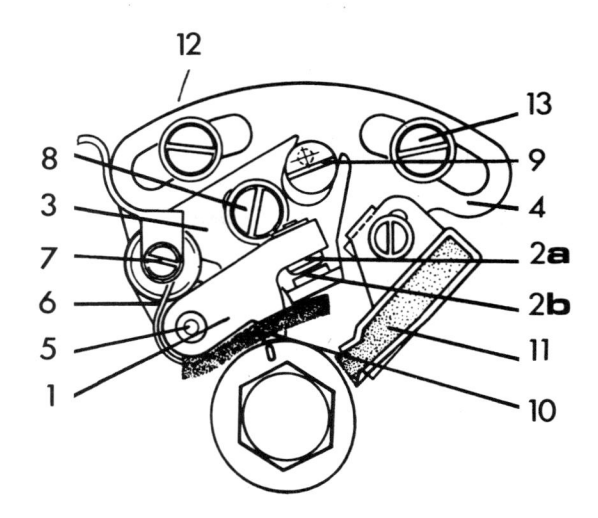

Fig. 3.1 Contact breaker and timing adjustment screws

1 Pivoted contact breaker
2a Pivoted point
2b Fixed point
3 Contact breaker plate
4 Back plate
5 Pivot pin
6 Spring
7 Connector screw
8 Fixing screw
9 Adjusting screw
10 Felt lubricator
11 Felt lubricator
12 Ignition timing setting screws
13 Ignition timing setting screws

Fig. 3.2a Timing light circuit using the machine's battery

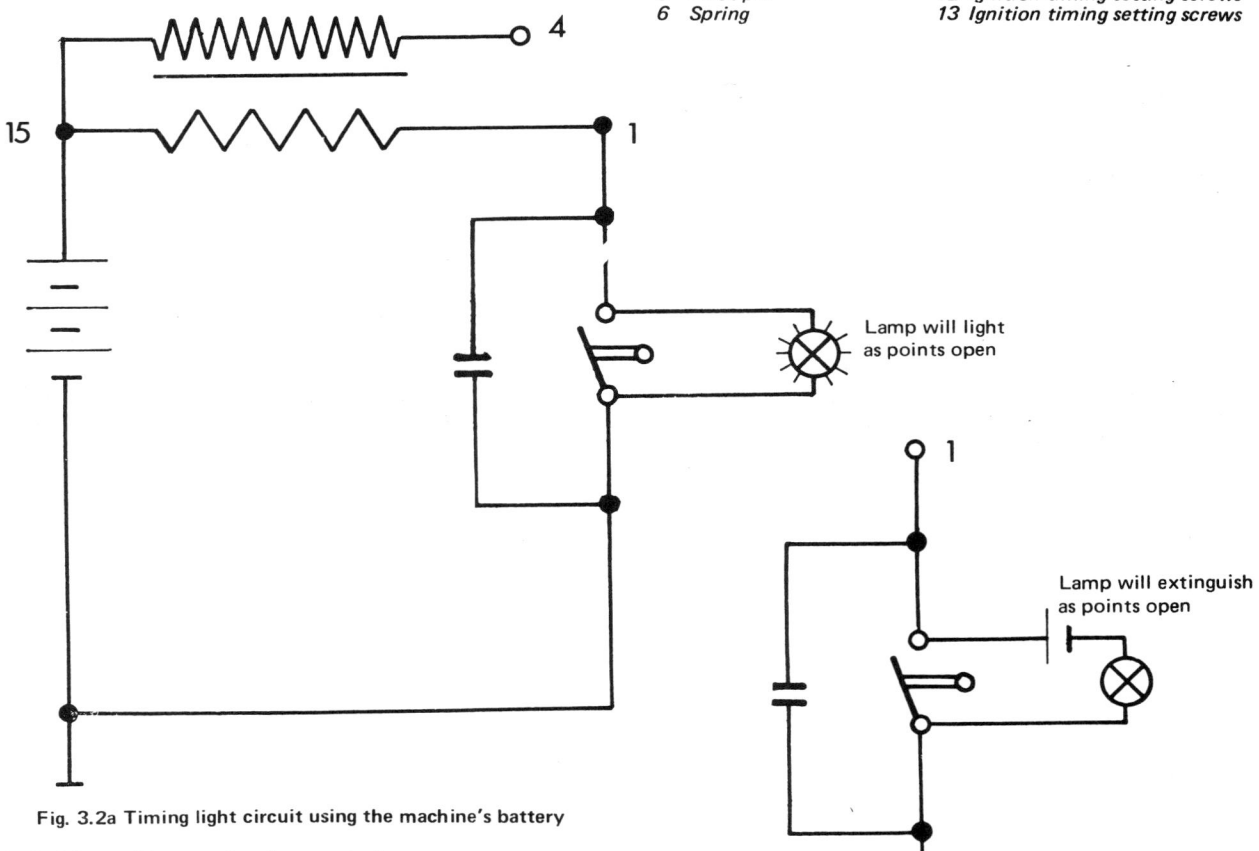

1 Ignition coil/contact breaker terminal
15 Ignition coil/battery terminal
4 Spark plug lead

Fig. 3.2b Timing light circuit using an external battery

1 Ignition coil/contact breaker terminal

7 Ignition timing

1 Set the contact breaker to the correct gap (see Section 6).
2 Remove the spark plug and fit a dial test indicator or the MZ setting gauge. If neither of these are available use a rule or vernier caliper, after first removing the cylinder head. Alternatively, a long piece of steel bar should be inserted through the plug hole; find TDC and mark the bar. Remove the bar and mark the correct ignition advance (see Specification) on the bar above the TDC mark. This bar can now be used as a timing gauge.
N.B. A dial test indicator or the steel bar timing device can be used only on the models that are fitted with a vertical spark plug. To use a dial test indicator on models fitted with an inclined plug, the cylinder head will have to be removed.
3 Connect a timing lamp as shown in Fig. 3.2a or 3.2b. When using Fig. 3.2a, the lamp will light when the contacts open. When using an external supply, as in Fig. 3.2b, the lamp will be extinguished when the contacts open.
4 Slacken the two screws retaining the contact breaker assembly and turn the crankshaft in the direction of normal rotation, ie; clockwise as viewed from the dynamo side, using the dynamo armature bolt. Set the crankshaft to the correct ignition setting BTDC (see Specification), and rotate the contact breaker assembly until the ignition lamp is either lit or extinguished, according to the method used. Tighten the two screws. Check that when tightening the screws the ignition timing has not altered. Reset if necessary.
N.B. On models fitted with an auto advance/retard mechanism, the timing must be carried out with the unit wedged open, ie; in the fully advanced position.
5 It cannot be over-stressed that the ignition timing must always be set to a high standard of accuracy if optimum performance is to be preserved. For this reason it is preferable to use the dial gauge method.

8 Spark plugs - checking and resetting the gaps

1 The ES models can be fitted with an NGK, B7HS or B7HV spark plug as standard, whilst the TS models should have the 'harder' B8HS or B8HV versions. Certain operating conditions may indicate a change in spark plug grade. The type recommended gives the best all-round service.
2 Check the gap of the plug points during every three monthly or fifteen hundred mile service. To reset the gap, bend the outer electrode to bring it closer to the centre electrode and check that a 0.5 mm feeler gauge can be inserted. Never bend the central electrode or the insulator will crack, causing engine damage if the particles fall in whilst the engine is running.
3 With some experience, the condition of the spark plug electrode and insulator can be used as a reliable guide to engine operating conditions. See accompanying diagram.
4 Beware of overtightening the spark plug, otherwise there is risk of stripping the thread from the aluminium alloy cylinder head. The plug should be sufficiently tight to sit firmly on the copper sealing washer, and no more. Use a spanner which is a good fit to prevent the spanner slipping and breaking the insulator.
5 If the thread in the cylinder head strips as a result of over-tightening the spark plug, it is possible to reclaim the head by use of a Helicoil thread insert. This is a cheap and convenient method of replacing the thread; most motorcycle dealers operate a service of this kind.
6 Make sure that the plug insulating cap is a good fit. It should also be kept clean to prevent tracking. The cap contains the suppressor that eliminate both radio and television interference.

9 Fault diagnosis - ignition system

Symptom	Cause	Remedy
Engine will not start	No spark at plug	Try replacement plug if gap correct. Check whether contact breaker points are opening and closing, also whether they are clean.
	Battery discharged	Check ignition switch and coil. Use emergency ignition switch position and bump start.
Engine starts but runs erratically	Intermittent or weak spark Incorrect ignition timing	Try replacement plug. Check condenser. Check accuracy of ignition timing. Low output from flywheel magneto generator or imminent breakdown of ignition coil. Fit replacement.
	Plug has whiskered Plug lead insulation breaking down	Check for breaks in outer covering.
Engine lacks power or overheats	Retarded ignition timing	Check timing and also contact breaker gap. Check auto. advance/retard mechanism is functioning (where fitted).
Engine misfires on high loads and/or high speeds	Weak spark Faulty plug	Check whole ignition system. Replace with a new plug.

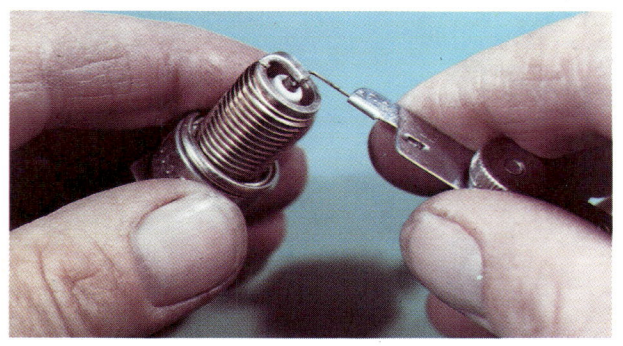

Spark plug maintenance: Checking plug gap with feeler gauges

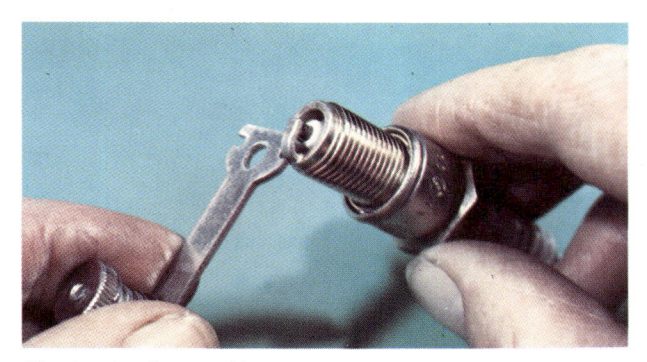

Altering the plug gap. Note use of correct tool

Spark plug conditions: A brown, tan or grey firing end is indicative of correct engine running conditions and the selection of the appropriate heat rating plug

White deposits have accumulated from excessive amounts of oil in the combustion chamber or through the use of low quality oil. Remove deposits or a hot spot may form

Black sooty deposits indicate an over-rich fuel/air mixture, or a malfunctioning ignition system. If no improvement is obtained, try one grade hotter plug

Wet, oily carbon deposits form an electrical leakage path along the insulator nose, resulting in a misfire. The cause may be a badly worn engine or a malfunctioning ignition system

A blistered white insulator or melted electrode indicates over-advanced ignition timing or a malfunctioning cooling system. If correction does not prove effective, try a colder grade plug

A worn spark plug not only wastes fuel but also overloads the whole ignition system because the increased gap requires higher voltage to initiate the spark. This condition can also affect air pollution

Chapter 4 Frame and forks

Contents

General description ... 1	telescopic forks ... 8
Telescopic front forks - removal from frame and dismantling ... 2	Swinging arm rear fork - removal ... 9
Telescopic front forks - examination and renovation ... 3	Swinging arm rear fork - examination, renovation and replacement ... 10
Telescopic front forks - replacement in frame ... 4	Suspension units - front (where applicable) and rear - removal, renovation and replacement ... 11
Earles type front forks - removal from frame and dismantling ... 5	Frame - examination and repair ... 12
Earles type front forks - examination, renovation and replacement ... 6	Speedometer and speedometer cable ... 13
Steering head bearings - telescopic front forks ... 7	Centre stand, prop stand and footrests - examination and maintenance ... 14
Steering head bearings - Earles type front forks and early	Fault diagnosis - frame and forks ... 15

Specifications

Telescopic front forks

Stanchion distortion limit	0.05 mm (0.002 in.) (or chrome plating worn through)
Top bush internal diameter	31.850 - 31.889 mm
Bottom bush internal diameter	37.875 - 37.900 mm
Slider internal diameter	38.00 - 38.05 mm
Oil capacity, each leg	220 cc

	ES150	TS150	ES250	TS250
Rake	61°	60°	63°	63°
Castor	95 mm	90 mm	105 mm	66 mm

Swinging arm
Bearing radial wear limit ... 0.1 mm (0.004 in.)

1 General description

Two basic types of frame are used, one being of the tubular or pressed steel diamond shaped type which is fitted to all models, except the TS250. This latter machine has a spine frame from which the engine is suspended.

Two types of front suspension system are fitted to the models covered by this manual, either the Earles fork type or conventional telescopic forks. A conventional swinging arm with adjustable rear suspension units is fitted to all models.

2 Telescopic front forks - removal from frame and dismantling

1 To service the front fork legs there is no necessity to completely remove both fork legs and yokes from the steering head of the frame. If this form of attention is required, proceed from paragraph 3 of this Section onwards.
2 To remove the forks as a complete unit, undo and remove the steering column domed nut and the two fork tube top nuts, after disconnecting the control cables at their handlebar levers. After lifting off the handlebars and upper yoke, it is possible to remove the forks complete with the bottom yoke mudguard and front wheel. To obtain sufficient clearance, it is easier to lay the bike on its side.
3 With the front wheel and mudguard removed, (see Chapter 5, Section 3 for the method of front wheel removal), unscrew the fork stanchion top nut. Slacken the pinch bolt in the bottom yoke and pull out the fork stanchion and slider complete. Repeat, if necessary, for the other fork leg.
4 Turn the fork leg upside down and drain off the damping oil. The fork leg spring will also come out as the fork leg is inverted.
5 Carefully remove the rubber dust cover using a screwdriver.
6 Unscrew the slider ring nut using a C-spanner and pull out the stanchion, bringing with it the top and bottom fork bushes and the damper valve assembly.
7 Slide the top bush off the fork stanchion, then remove the lower circlip and slide off the bottom bush.
8 If required, the damping valve assembly can be detached by removing the wire circlip.
9 Dismantle each fork leg separately, so that there is no risk of inadvertently interchanging parts.

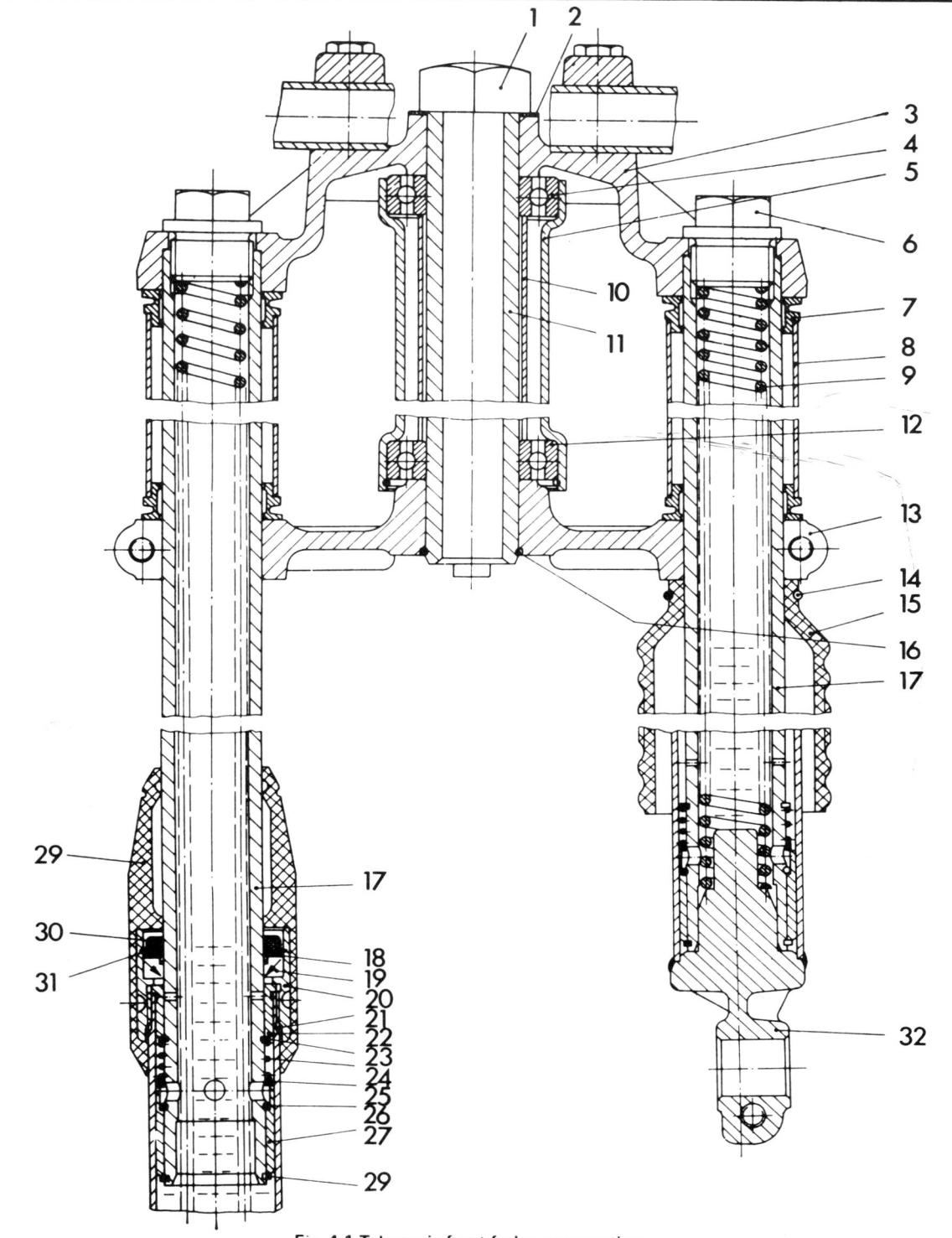

Fig. 4.1 Telescopic front forks: cross section

Left-hand side extended

1. Steering column nut
2. Lock washer
3. Top yoke
4. Ball bearing 6006
5. Frame steering head
6. Top nut
7. Rubber ring for headlamp bracket
8. Headlamp bracket
9. Spring
10. Spacer
11. Steering column tube
12. Ball bearing 6006
13. Bottom yoke
14. Circlip
15. Gaiter
16. Circlip

Right-hand side compressed

17. Stanchion
18. Support ring
19. Seal
20. Slide nut
21. Slider
22. Upper bush
23. Circlip
24. Damping valve spring
25. Damping valve ring
26. Circlip
27. Bottom bush
28. Circlip
29. Gaiter
30. Felt seal holder
31. Felt
32. Wheel spindle bush

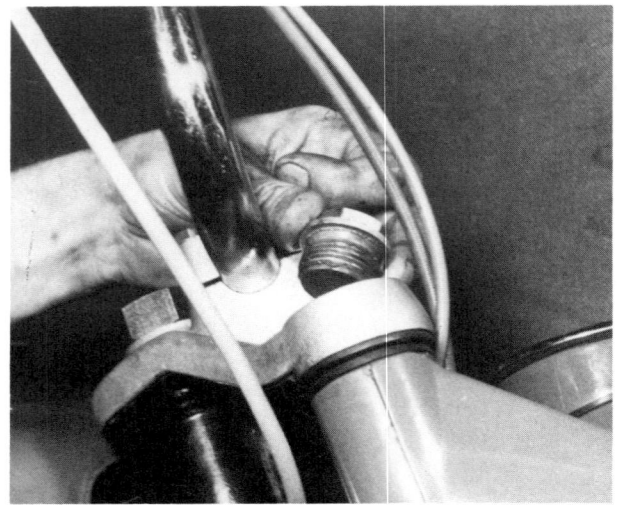

2.2 Unscrew the fork top nuts (TS150)

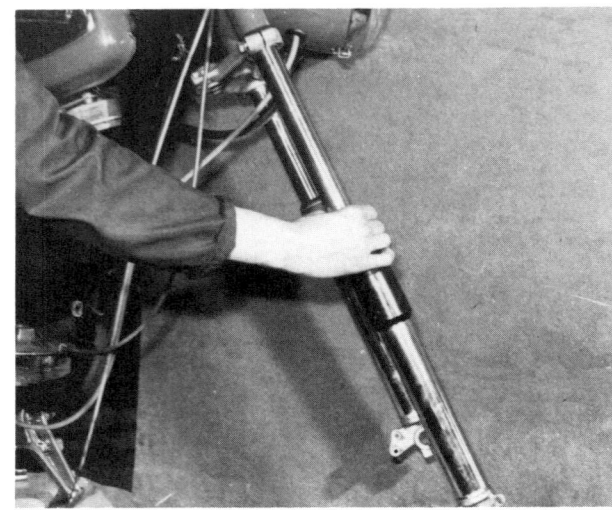

2.4 Pull out the complete fork leg

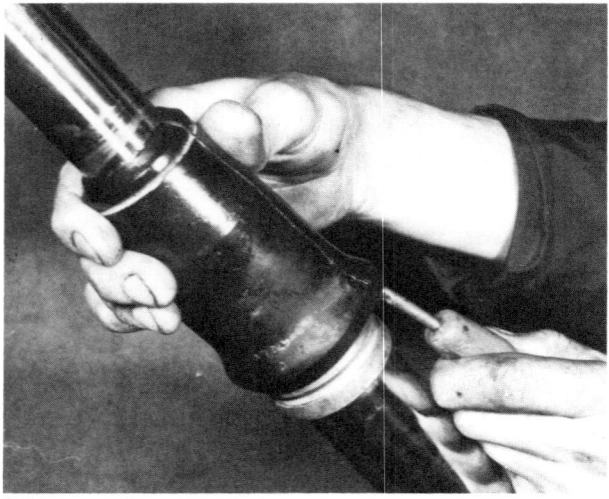

2.5 Remove the rubber dust cover

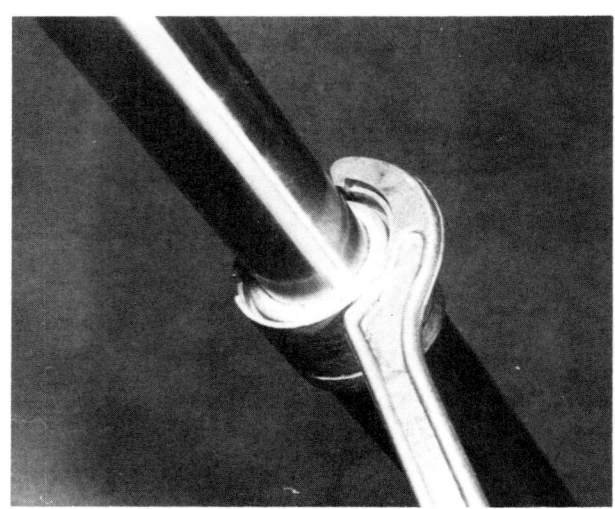

2.6 Use a C-spanner to undo the slider nut and ...

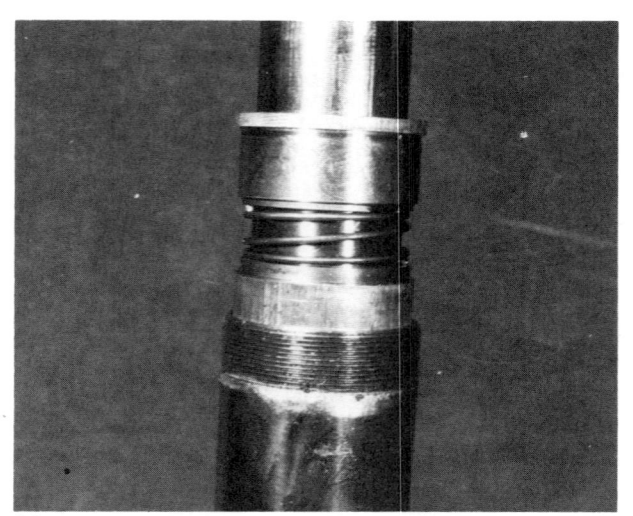

2.6a ... pull out the stanchion complete with top bush

2.7 Lift off the top bush

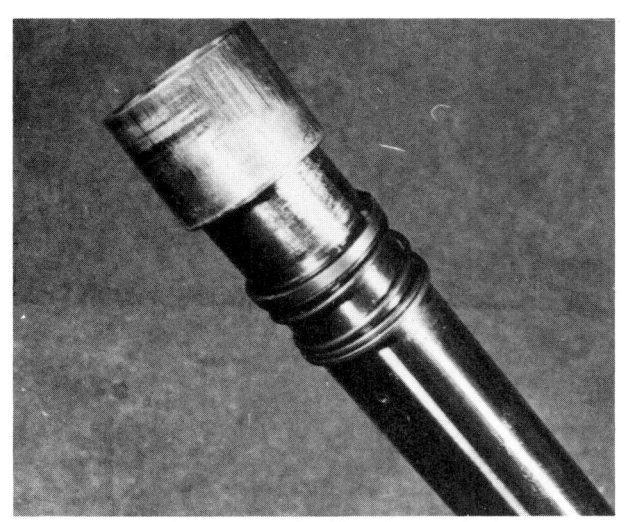

2.7a Remove the circlip and lift off the bottom bush

2.8 The damper valve is retained by a wire circlip

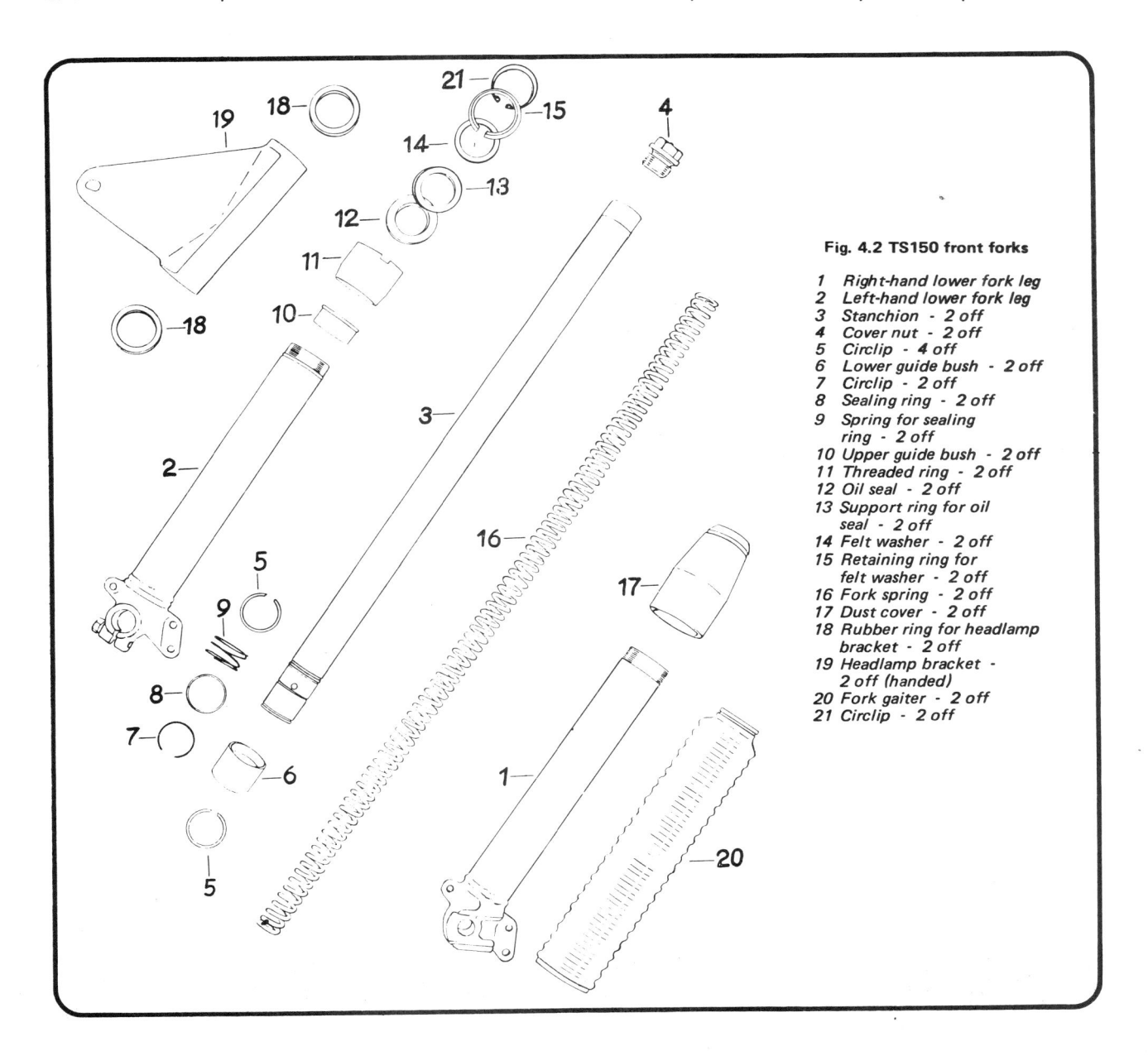

Fig. 4.2 TS150 front forks

1 Right-hand lower fork leg
2 Left-hand lower fork leg
3 Stanchion - 2 off
4 Cover nut - 2 off
5 Circlip - 4 off
6 Lower guide bush - 2 off
7 Circlip - 2 off
8 Sealing ring - 2 off
9 Spring for sealing ring - 2 off
10 Upper guide bush - 2 off
11 Threaded ring - 2 off
12 Oil seal - 2 off
13 Support ring for oil seal - 2 off
14 Felt washer - 2 off
15 Retaining ring for felt washer - 2 off
16 Fork spring - 2 off
17 Dust cover - 2 off
18 Rubber ring for headlamp bracket - 2 off
19 Headlamp bracket - 2 off (handed)
20 Fork gaiter - 2 off
21 Circlip - 2 off

Chapter 4: Frame and forks

3 Telescopic front forks - examination and renovation

1 See the Specifications Section at the beginning of this Chapter for all bush dimensions and wear limits.
2 Check the condition of the fork bushes. If they are scored or worn, renew them.
3 Check that the damper valve ring is free to move on the fork stanchion. Also check the fork stanchion where it slides in the top bush as this is the most likely place for wear and scoring to occur.
4 Roll the fork stanchions on a flat surface to check that they are not bent.
5 Check the length of the fork springs against each other. If there is a noticeable difference, renew the pair.
6 Check the condition of the felt seal located under a supporting washer in the fork slider nut. Also check the rubber oil seal. Renew them if the forks have been leaking or if in doubt about their condition.
7 Reassemble the fork legs using the reverse procedure to dismantling, after having thoroughly cleaned and lightly oiled all the components. Use the recommended grade of fork oil for this purpose.

4 Telescopic front forks - replacement in frame

1 Refill the fork legs with the correct volume and grade of oil.
2 Replace the fork legs in the reverse order to removal. Use a little sealing compound on the stanchion top nuts and tighten them down to a torque wrench setting of 29 lb ft. Operate the forks several times before tightening their bottom yoke pinch bolts, to align the fork legs correctly.

5 Earles type front forks - removal from frame and dismantling

1 It is unlikely, except in the case of accident damage, that it will be necessary to remove the front forks completely. However, this is achieved by removing the steering column top nut, and then dismantling the steering head bearings, as described in Section 8 of this Chapter, after disconnecting the control cables at their handlebar levers. It is now possible to remove the forks, mudguard and front wheel as a complete unit. To obtain sufficient clearance it is preferable to lay the bike on its side.
2 Remove the front wheel as described in Chapter 5, Section 3.
3 Remove the bottom bolt in each of the suspension units.
4 Remove the locknut and nut from the pivot spindle opposite end to grease nipple.
5 Remove the two bolts in the rear of the fork carrier and pull out the pivot spindle.
6 The front swinging arm is now free to be removed. Note the position of the washers and oil seals.

6 Earles type front forks - examination, renovation and replacement

1 Check the condition of the bushes in the swinging arm and renew them if necessary. Press out the old bushes using a bench vice and spacing collar (a socket from a socket drive set will suffice). Press in the replacement.
2 Check and renew the rubber seals if necessary.
3 Check that the pivot spindle is not bent, by rolling it on a flat surface. Also examine the bearing surfaces for wear or damage. Renew if necessary.
4 Whilst the pivot spindle is out, pump out all the old grease with new, making sure that the grease-ways are clear. Renew the rubber 'O' rings, where fitted.
5 Replace the swinging arm using the reverse procedure to removal. Make sure to fit the dust cap between the swinging arm and carrier and to locate the machined flats of the pivot spindle

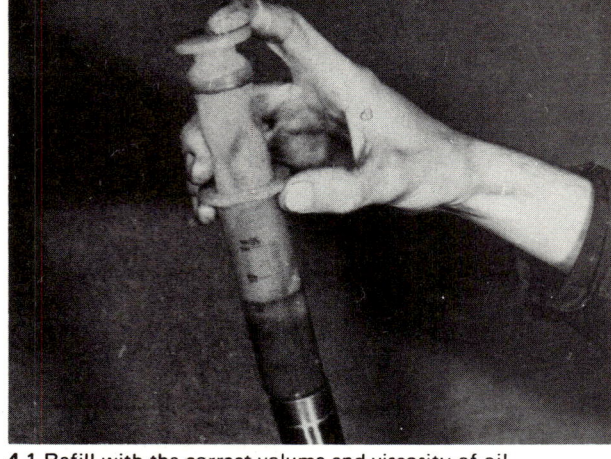

4.1 Refill with the correct volume and viscosity of oil

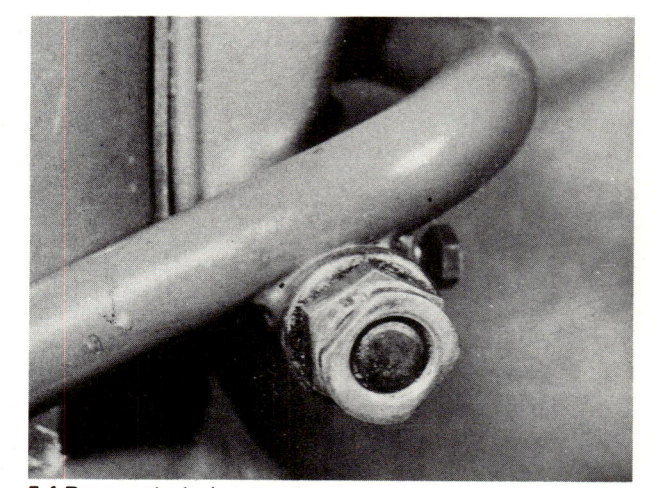

5.4 Remove the lock nut and nut

5.5 Remove the two locking bolts and ...

Chapter 4: Frame and forks

5.5a Drift out the spindle

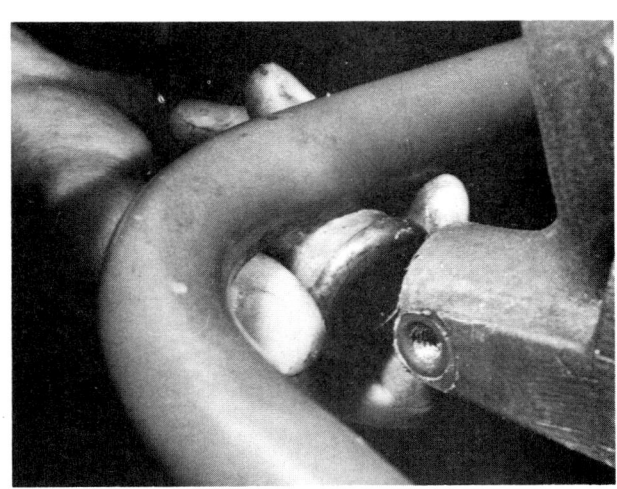

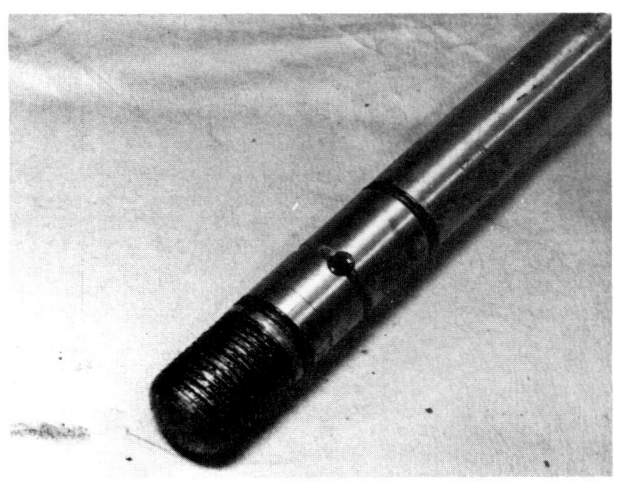

6.4 Remove the rubber O-ring

5.6 Note the position of all dust caps and ...

5.6a ... washers

in the correct position for clamping by the two bolts.

6 When reassembled, pump in fresh grease until it just emerges from each bearing.

7 Steering head bearings - telescopic front forks

1 A pair of ball journal bearings are fitted and should not require adjustment.

2 To regrease or remove the bearings, first detach the front forks complete, (see Section 2) and drift out the bearings. Note that the bottom bearing is retained by a circlip.

3 The only adjustment required on reassembly is to tighten down the steering column domed nut to a torque wrench setting of 108 lb ft. This should be accomplished before tightening the pinch bolts in the bottom yoke.

8 Steering head bearings - Earles type front forks and early telescopic forks

1 Two cup and cone bearings, each with twenty two, 6.35 mm (¼ in.) ball bearings are used in the steering head assembly.

2 Access to the steering head bearings is by removing the handlebar cover or lock plate.

3 If it is desired to completely remove the steering column, bend back the lockwasher and remove the steering column ring nut with a C-spanner. This allows the steering column and complete front fork assembly to be withdrawn from the frame.

4 Clean and examine the cups and cones of the bearings. They should have a polished appearance and show no signs of indentation. Renew the whole set, if necessary.

5 Clean and examine the ball bearings which should also be polished and show no signs of surface cracks or blemishes. If any require renewal the whole set must be replaced.

6 To hold the ball bearings in position during reassembly, pack the bearings with grease. Note that there should be enough space left to insert one extra bearing. This space is necessary to prevent the bearings from skidding on each other.

7 Do not over-tighten the ring nut, or the bearings will be damaged. As a guide, only a very slight pressure should be needed to start the front wheel turning to either side under its own weight, when it is raised clear of the ground. Check that the bearings are not too slack by trying to move the forks in a forwards and backwards direction. There should be no discernible movement. It is quite easy to place a loading of several tons on the bearings quite inadvertently, and find the handlebars will still turn with relative ease.

Chapter 4: Frame and forks

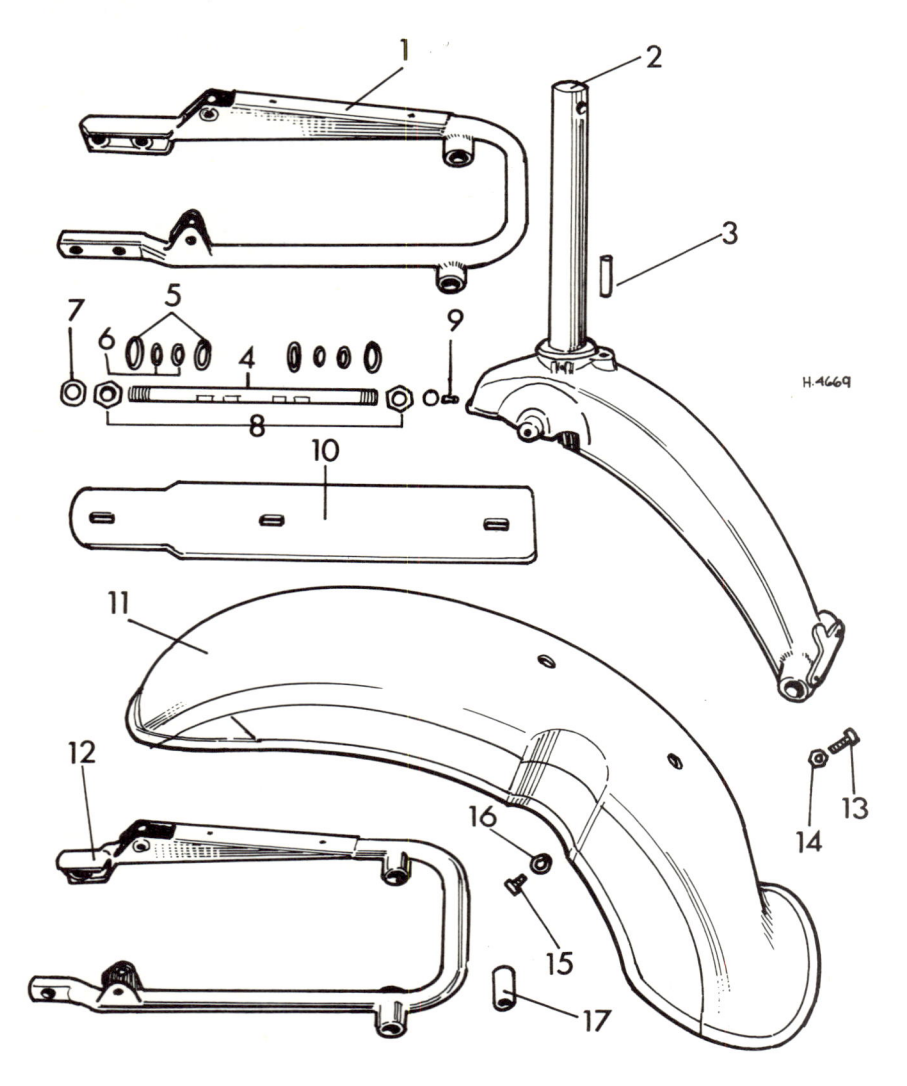

Fig. 4.3 Front fork carrier and front swinging arm (Earles type)

1. Swinging arm (sidecar design)
2. Front fork carrier and steering head column
3. Stud
4. Swinging arm pivot spindle
5. Protective cap and washer - 2 off
6. Rubber sealing ring - 4 off
7. Lock nut
8. Nut M8 x 1.5 - 2 off
9. Grease nipple
10. Mudguard mounting rubber
11. Front mudguard
12. Swinging arm (solo design)
13. Bolt M8 - 2 off
14. Nut M8 - 2 off
15. Bolt M8 - 3 off
16. Washer, spring and plain - 3 off
17. Bush

9 Swinging arm rear fork - removal

1 Remove the rear wheel as described in Chapter 5, Section 7.
2 Disconnect the rear chain at the spring link. It is not necessary to remove the rear wheel sprocket carrier. Undo the speedometer cable from the rear wheel sprocket, where applicable.
3 Remove the locknuts from the pivot spindle at the end opposite to the grease nipple.
4 Remove the two bolts in the rear of the pivot bearing and pull out the pivot spindle. The swinging arm fork can now be withdrawn rearwards. Note the position and arrangement of the washers and dust seals.

10 Swinging arm rear fork - examination, renovation and replacement

1 Use a similar procedure to that described for the Earles type front forks (see Section 6 of this Chapter).

2 Replace the swinging arm by reversing the dismantling procedure. Some difficulty may be experienced if the rear engine mountings have sprung open. If this has occurred, clamp the mounting with a G-clamp before replacing the swinging arm.
3 If the engine has been removed, the engine mountings will also be free and the bushes should be checked and renewed if worn. Make sure that all washers and seals are replaced.

11 Suspension units - front (where applicable) and rear - removal, renovation and replacement

1 The front suspension units fitted to the Earles type front forks are non-adjustable.
2 The rear suspension units on all models are adjustable by means of an alloy lever. When adjusting them, make sure that both levers are on the same setting. The hardest setting is with the levers pointing forwards. Only two settings are possible.
3 To remove the suspension units, undo both the top and bottom fixing bolts and knock the units out from the swinging arm.

Chapter 4: Frame and forks

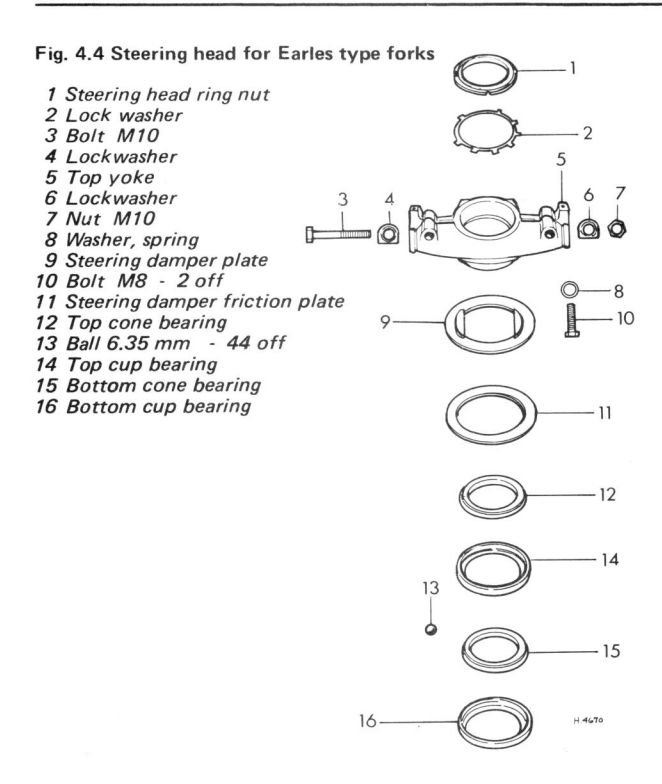

Fig. 4.4 Steering head for Earles type forks

1 Steering head ring nut
2 Lock washer
3 Bolt M10
4 Lockwasher
5 Top yoke
6 Lockwasher
7 Nut M10
8 Washer, spring
9 Steering damper plate
10 Bolt M8 - 2 off
11 Steering damper friction plate
12 Top cone bearing
13 Ball 6.35 mm - 44 off
14 Top cup bearing
15 Bottom cone bearing
16 Bottom cup bearing

9.3 Lift out the swinging arm ...

4 To remove the springs, each unit should be held in a vice and the spring tension collar, (rear units only), set at the softest position. With one person pushing down on the spring, a second person should remove the split collets from the top. The spring can now be lifted off. Repeat for the second unit.

5 Check the length of the springs against each other and if there is an appreciable difference, renew them as a pair to ensure even tension.

6 Check the damper units for leakage of fluid and also the damping action by pulling and pushing the damper rod in and out of the unit whilst holding it in a vertical position. An even resistance should be felt with no sudden easy movement. If one unit is defective in this respect, always renew both units so that an even matching is obtained.

7 It is possible to fully dismantle some units. This is, however, inadvisable since the units have to be set up and regulated as a matched pair, which is a specialised job.

8 There are two rubber bushes fitted to each suspension unit, one at each end. Renew them if they show signs of wear and/or have perished. They should be pressed out and new ones pressed in (see Section 6.1 of this Chapter).

9 Assemble and replace the suspension units in the reverse order of dismantling.

12 Frame - examination and repair

1 The frame is unlikely to require attention unless an accident has caused damage. In this case the frame should be taken to a specialist for repair, or preferably be renewed.

2 It is wise to check the frame occasionally for cracks especially around the welded sections and those subjected to vibration and stress eg; footrest mounting lugs. Rust corrosion can also lead to defects and should be eliminated in its early stages.

3 A frame which is out of alignment will cause handling problems. If this is suspected, it is usually necessary to remove all the components so that the bare frame can be checked and possibly realigned by a specialist in this type of work.

13 Speedometer and speedometer cable

1 The speedometer head is driven by a flexible cable. No repair is possible and an exchange or replacement unit must be obtained.

2 If the instrument fails, first check the cable. Also check the cable is the instrument gives a jerky response, since the cable is probably dry or kinked.

3 To examine the inner cable, unscrew the cable nut and withdraw it. Check for fraying, kinks or worn squares on the ends. Renew if necessary. Before replacing the inner cable, check that the cable outer is not damaged or chaffed, since damage of this nature will greatly shorten the life of the new replacement.

4 When replacing the inner cable, lightly grease it, except for the last six inches near the instrument head. This will help to prevent grease working its way into the head and causing it to malfunction.

5 The speedometer drive mechanism is unlikely to cause trouble and is covered in Chapter 5, Section 14.3, for the ES250 model and Chapter 5, Section 14.2, for all models fitted with a rear wheel driven speedometer.

14 Centre stand, prop stand and footrests - examination and maintenance

1 The centre and prop stands require little attention except for the occasional greasing. A check should be made on the tightness of their securing bolts and condition of their return springs. Renew the springs if in doubt about their condition, since a falling stand, particularly in the case of the prop stand, can cause an accident whilst cornering.

2 If the footrests get bent, if, for example, the machine is dropped, they can be straightened quite easily. It is best to remove the footrest from the machine so as not to place any strain on the mountings. Bend it straight whilst heating it to a dull red heat with a blow lamp. Do not forget to remove the footrest rubber, before applying heat.

9.3a ...noting the position of the thrust washers (ES250)

9.3b ...on the outside and the inside

10.3 The rear engine mounting bracket

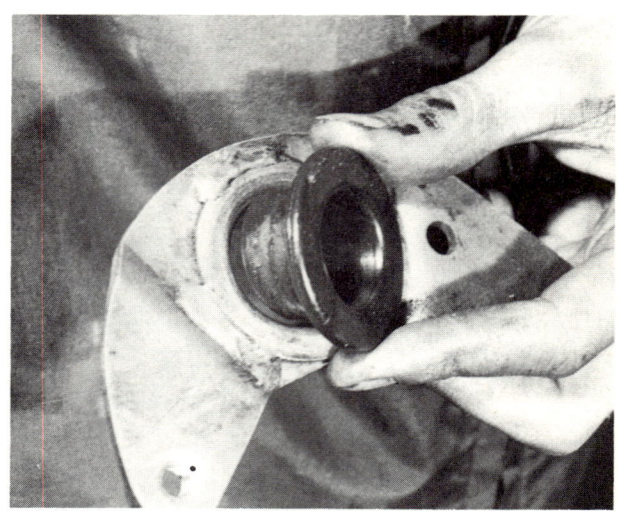

10.3a Check the condition of the inner mounting bushes and ...

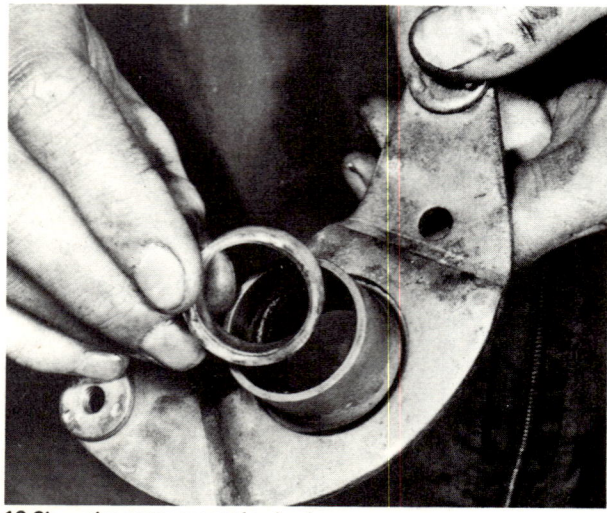

10.3b ... the outer mounting bushes

11.4 Press down the spring and remove the split collet

Chapter 4: Frame and forks

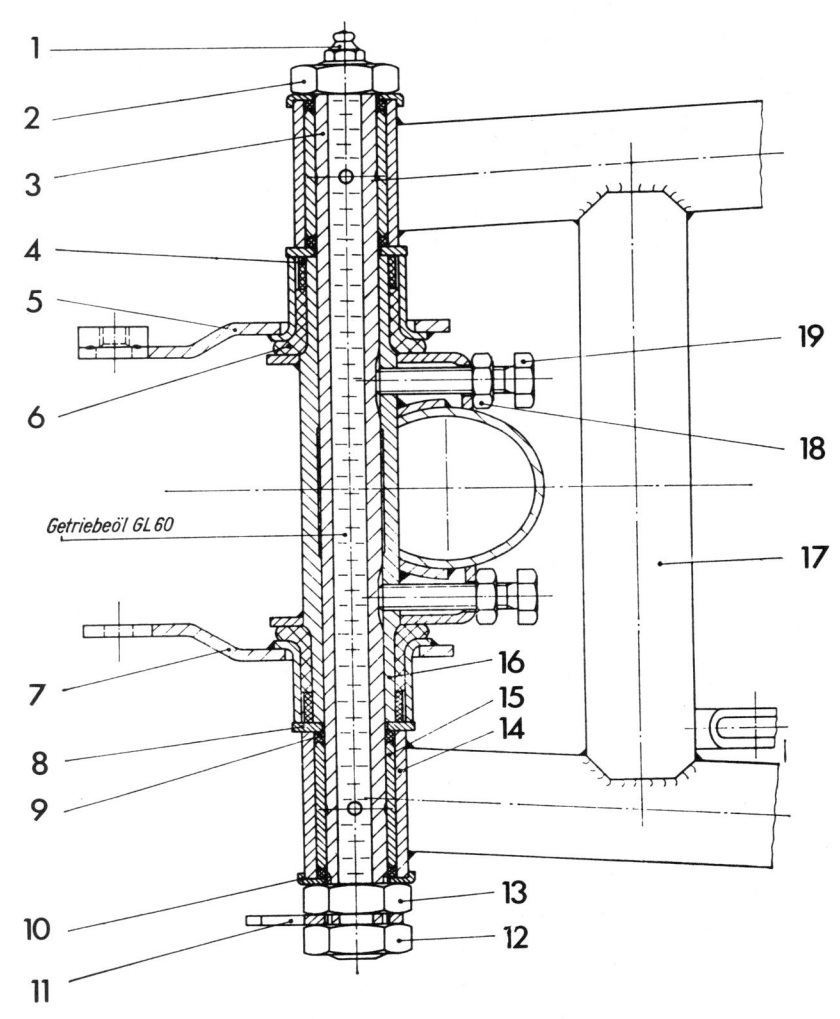

1. Grease nipple
2. Nut M18 x 1.5
3. Pivot spindle
4. Spacer
5. Right-hand engine mounting plate
6. Engine mounting bush
7. Left-hand engine mounting plate
8. Thrust washer
9. Rubber sealing ring
10. Protective cap
11. Prop stand spring plate (TS250 only)
12. Lock nut
13. Adjusting nut
14. Swinging arm bearing tube
15. Swinging arm bush
16. Frame pivot spindle tube
17. Rear swinging arm
18. Lock nut
19. Clamping bolt

Fig. 4.5 Rear swinging arm fork and engine mountings: cross section

15 Fault diagnosis - frame and forks

Symptom	Cause	Remedy
Machine is unduly sensitive to road conditions	Forks and/or rear suspension units have defective damping	Check oil level in forks. Replace rear suspension units.
Machine tends to roll at low speeds	Steering head bearings overtight or damaged	Slacken bearing adjustment. If no improvement, dismantle and inspect bearings.
Machine tends to wander, steering is imprecise	Worn swinging arm bearings	Check and if necessary renew bearings.
Fork action stiff	Fork legs have twisted in yokes or have been drawn together at lower ends	Slacken off spindle nut clamps, pinch bolts in fork yokes and fork top nuts. Pump forks several times before retightening from bottom.
Forks judder when front brake is applied	Worn fork bushes Steering head bearings too slack	Strip forks and replace bushes. Readjust, to take up play (Earles forks only).
Wheels out of alignment	Frame distorted as result of accident damage	Check frame alignment after stripping out. If bent, specialist repair is necessary.

Chapter 5 Wheels, brakes and tyres

Contents

General description ... 1	Stop lamp switch - adjustment ... 11
Front wheel - examination and renovation ... 2	Rear wheel sprocket and carrier - removal, examination
Front wheel - removal and replacement ... 3	and replacement ... 12
Front wheel - removing the bearings ... 4	Cush drive ... 13
Front brake - examination, renovation and reassembly ... 5	Speedometer drive ... 14
Rear wheel - examination and renovation ... 6	Rear wheel sprocket ... 15
Rear wheel - removal and replacement ... 7	Final drive chain - examination and lubrication ... 16
Rear wheel - removing the bearings ... 8	Tyres - removal and replacement ... 17
Rear brake - examination, renovation and reassembly ... 9	Fault diagnosis - wheels, brakes and tyres ... 18
Front and rear brake - adjustment ... 10	

Specifications

	ES150	TS150	ES250	TS250
Tyres				
Size - Front ins. ...	3.00 x 18	2.75 x 18	3.25 x 16 or 3.00 x 16	3.00 x 16
- Rear ins. ...	3.00 x 18	3.00 x 18	3.50 x 16	3.50 x 16
Brakes				
Front and rear:				
Diameter - mm ...	150 (5.9 in.)	160 front (6.3 in.) 150 rear (5.9 in.)	160 (6.3 in.)	160 (6.3 in.)
Width - mm ...	30 (1.18 in.)	30 (1.18 in.)	30 (1.18 in.)	30 (1.18 in.)
Chain				
Size ...	½ x ¼ in.	½ x ¼ in.	½ x 5/16 in.	½ x 5/16 in.
No. of links ...	120	120	118	126
Sprocket size (teeth):				
Gearbox ...	15/16	16	21	21
Rear wheel ...	48	48	45	47
Tyre pressure - all models p.s.i.				
Front ...	22	22	22	22
Rear* ...	28	28	28	28

*Increase to 31 p.s.i. when carrying a passenger.

1 General description

Both wheels of the 150 models are of 18 inch diameter while those of the 250 models are of 16 inch diameter. A ribbed front tyre and block tread rear tyre are fitted as standard. The tyre section varies with the different models.

All brakes are of the single leading shoe pattern. An unusual feature is that the stop lamp switch is integral with the rear brake plate. The rear wheel sprocket incorporates a rubber cush drive arrangement on all models.

The speedometer drive is from the rear hub except on the ES250 model, where the drive is taken from the engine sprocket. The rear wheel is of the q/d type ie; there is no need to detach the final drive chain when removing the rear wheel.

2 Front wheel - examination and renovation

1 Place the machine on the centre stand so that the front wheel is raised clear of the ground. Spin the wheel and check for rim alignment. Small irregularities can be corrected by tightening the

spokes in the affected area, although a certain amount of experience is necessary if over-correction is to be avoided. Any 'flats' in the wheel rim should be evident at the same time. These are more difficult to remove with any success and in most cases the wheel will need to be rebuilt on a new rim. Apart from the effect on stability, there is greater risk of damage to the tyre bead and walls if the machine is run with a deformed wheel.

2 Check for loose or broken spokes. Tapping the spokes is the best guide to tension. A loose spoke will produce a quite different note and should be tightened by turning the nipple in an anti-clockwise direction. Always check for run-out by spinning the wheel again.

3 Front wheel - removal and replacement

1 Place the machine on its centre stand and support it so that the front wheel is clear of the ground and the bike will not tip forwards when the wheel is removed.
2 Undo the wheel spindle nut and remove it along with the washer. On models with telescopic front forks, slacken the pinch bolt at the bottom of the left-hand fork leg first.
3 Pull out the wheel spindle. If it is tight, gently tap it out with a suitable drift.
4 Lift the wheel out of the forks, leaving the brake plate assembly suspended by the Bowden cable.
5 Lift off the hub cover, from the left-hand side of the hub.
6 When replacing the wheel, follow the procedure in reverse. Do not forget to fit the grease seal, and make sure the lug on the brake plate engages correctly in the forks. Unless the brake plate is firmly anchored, the brake will jam in the 'full on' position immediately it is applied and cause a skid that may result in a serious accident.
7 Before finally tightening the wheel spindle nut, spin the wheel and operate the front brake to centralise the linings in the drum.
8 If the machine is fitted with telescopic front forks, operate the forks a couple of times before tightening the pinch bolt. This procedure will ensure that the fork legs are parallel to each other.

4 Front wheel - removing the bearings

1 Remove the front wheel as described in the previous Section.
2 Remove both the oil seals. The bearings are removed by drifting both of them outwards. There is a spacing sleeve fitted between the bearings, which are of identical type.
3 Remove all the old grease from the hub and bearings, giving the latter a final wash in petrol. Check each bearing for play or signs of roughness when they are rotated. If there is any doubt about their condition, renew the bearings as a pair.
4 Repack the bearings with a high melting point grease. Repack the hub centre with grease, but do not fill. Allow plenty of space for the expansion of the grease when it is hot.
5 Drift in the bearings, using a soft drift on the outside ring of the bearing. Do not drift the centre ring otherwise damage will be incurred. Do not forget the spacing sleeve. Replace the oil seals, renewing them if necessary.

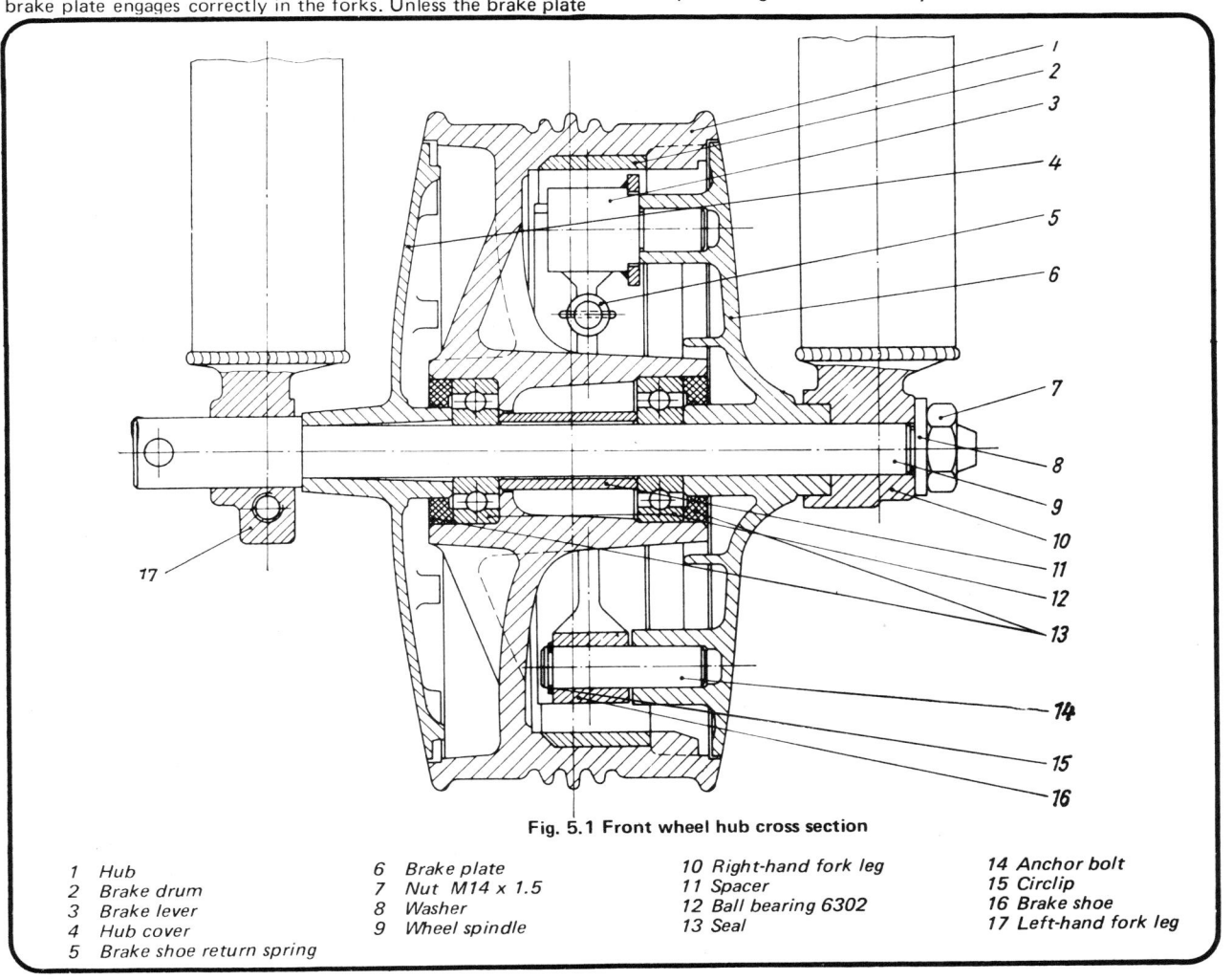

Fig. 5.1 Front wheel hub cross section

1 Hub
2 Brake drum
3 Brake lever
4 Hub cover
5 Brake shoe return spring
6 Brake plate
7 Nut M14 x 1.5
8 Washer
9 Wheel spindle
10 Right-hand fork leg
11 Spacer
12 Ball bearing 6302
13 Seal
14 Anchor bolt
15 Circlip
16 Brake shoe
17 Left-hand fork leg

Chapter 5: Wheels, brakes and tyres

3.3 Slacken the pinch bolt and drift out the spindle

3.5 Lift off the hub cover. Note the oil seal

3.6 The brake plate lug must align with the fork leg

4.2 Remove the oil seal

4.3 An example of a neglected wheel bearing

5 Front brake - examination, renovation and reassembly

1 Remove the front wheel as described in Section 3 of this Chapter and unhook the cable from the operating arm on the inside of the brake plate assembly.
2 Examine the condition of the brake linings. If they are worn they should be renewed.
3 The brake shoes are held in position by two circlips which, when removed, allow the shoes and cam to be lifted off the brake plate.
4 Dust out the drum and check that it is not scored or ridged. If it is damaged it will have to be skimmed in a lathe by a specialist. Dust off the brake plate.
5 When renewing the linings it is good policy to renew the return spring at the same time.
6 Before reassembly, lightly grease all the pivot points with a high melting point grease.
7 Reassemble by reversing the above procedure. Do not forget to replace the two circlips.

Chapter 5: Wheels, brakes and tyres

5.3 Remove the two circlips and ...

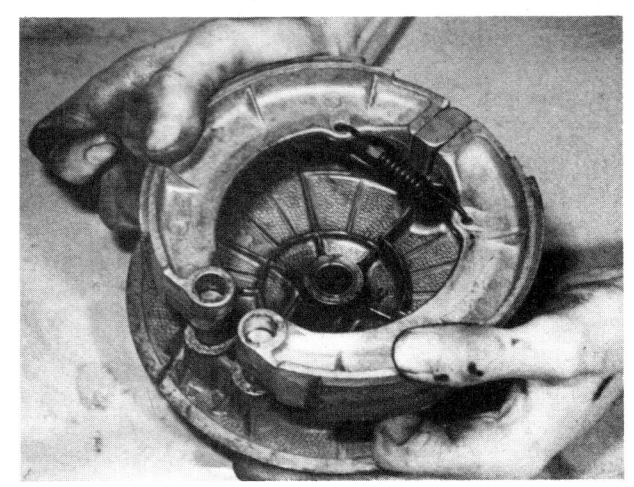

5.3a ... lift off the brake shoes

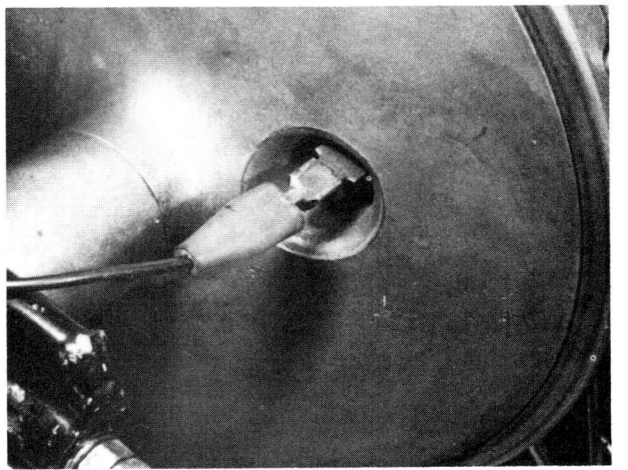

7.3 Remove the stop lamp lead

7.4 Remove wing nut to disconnect rear brake (ES250)

6 Rear wheel - examination and renovation

1 Use the same procedure as that adopted for the front wheel (see Section 2 of this Chapter).

7 Rear wheel - removal and replacement

1 The rear wheel is of the q/d type permitting it to be removed without disturbing the final drive chain.
2 Place the machine on its centre stand and support it so that the rear wheel is clear of the ground and the bike will not tip backwards when the wheel is removed.
3 Disconnect the stop light switch cable.
4 On ES250 models, disconnect the rear brake operating rod by unscrewing the adjusting nut.
5 Remove the torque arm bolt at the brake plate end.
6 Unscrew the wheel spindle and withdraw it. Remove the spacer if it has not already fallen out.
7 The wheel is now ready to be removed. Move it over to the left to free it from the cush drive rubber.
8 Replace the rear wheel by reversing the above procedure. Do not forget to reconnect the torque arm and tighten the bolt. Spin the wheel and operate the brake to centralise the linings before finally tightening the wheel spindle.

8 Rear wheel - removing the bearings

1 Remove the rear wheel as described in the previous Section and follow the procedure given for removal of the front wheel bearings (see Section 4). Note, however, that there is a further bearing fitted in the sprocket carrier, removal of which is covered in Section 12 of this Chapter.

9 Rear brake - examination, renovation and reassembly

1 Follow the procedure adopted for the front brake (see Section 5 of this Chapter).

7.5 Undo the torque arm bolt

7.6 Drift out the spindle

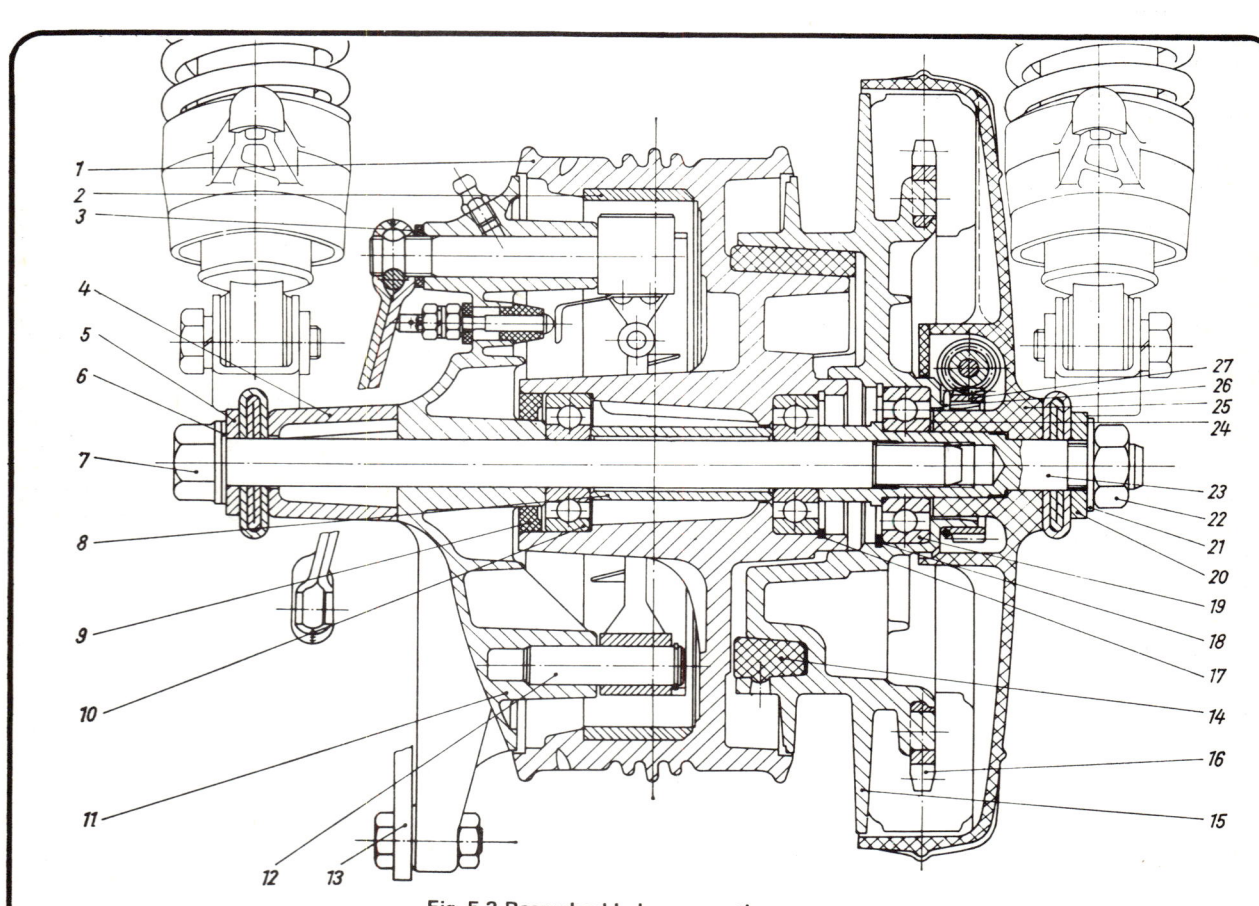

Fig. 5.2 Rear wheel hub cross section

1 Hub
2 Brake drum
3 Rubber seal
4 Spring sleeve
5 Left-hand rear wheel adjuster
6 Washer
7 Wheel spindle
8 Spacing sleeve
9 Seal
10 Ball bearing 6302
11 Brake plate
12 Anchor bolt
13 Torque arm
14 Cush drive rubber
15 Sprocket carrier
16 Sprocket
17 Circlip
18 Circlip
19 Ball bearing 6204
20 Right-hand rear wheel adjuster
21 Washer
22 Nut M14 x 1.5
23 Sprocket carrier spindle
24 Washer
25 Plastic chain cover
26 Circlip
27 Speedometer drive gear

Chapter 5: Wheels, brakes and tyres

10 Front and rear brake - adjustment

1 The front brake is adjusted by means of the handlebar lever adjuster.
2 The rear brake is adjusted by the wing nut on the rod operated version and by the adjuster at the brake plate end on the cable operated type.
3 After adjusting the brakes check that the linings are not binding by rotating the respective wheels.
4 After adjusting the rear brake, check the setting of the stop light switch (see following Section).

11 Stop lamp switch - adjustment

1 Adjustment of the stop lamp switch will probably be required if the rear brake has been adjusted.
2 Slacken the locknut of the switch adjusting screw and turn on the ignition.
3 Operate the rear brake pedal until the brake lining just contacts the drum, the point of contact being checked by rotating the rear wheel. Hold the brake pedal in this position and turn the slotted screw until the stop lamp is lit. Tighten the locknut and recheck the setting. Do not overtighten the locknut.

12 Rear wheel sprocket and carrier - removal, examination and replacement

1 The rear wheel sprocket carrier contains a separate ball bearing and the cush drive rubber. It also houses the speedometer drive except on the ES250 models where the drive is located on the engine sprocket.
2 Remove the rear wheel as described in Section 7.
3 Pull back the chain gaiter and disconnect the chain at its spring link. Pull the chain clear of the rear wheel sprocket.
4 Disconnect the speedometer drive cable, where applicable, by undoing the knurled nut and pulling the cable out.
5 Undo the large nut holding the carrier in the swinging arm and lift the unit out.
6 For models fitted with a rear wheel speedometer drive continue with paragraphs 7 to 10 and 14. For ES250 models continue with paragraphs 11 to 14.

All models except ES250
7 Lift off the plastic cover which contains part of the speedometer drive worm gear.
8 Drift out the spindle. Note the washer fitted in the worm gear side and the washer fitted between the spindle and bearing.
9 The bearing can be drifted out after having removed its circlip. Clean, check and refit the bearing using a similar procedure to that described in Sections 4.3 to 4.5.
10 Regrease the speedometer drive gear and replace the plastic cover.

ES250 model only
11 Lift off the plastic cover and drift out the spindle. Note the washer fitted in the oil seal.
12 The bearing can be drifted out after having removed the circlip. Clean, check and refit the bearing, using a similar procedure to that described in Sections 4.3 to 4.5.
13 Renew the oil seal if necessary and replace the plastic cover.
14 Replace the sprocket carrier and chain by reversing the removal procedure. Make sure to fit the spring link with its closed end facing the direction of travel.

13 Cush drive

1 Access to the cush drive rubber is obtained by removing the rear wheel sprocket carrier (see previous Section).
2 To remove the rubber on the ES250 models, the sprocket retaining bolts have to be detached. On the ES150 models there

12.4 Disconnect the speedometer cable (TS150)

12.7 The speedometer drive mechanism

12.8 Remove the thrust washer and ...

12.8a ... drift out the spindle

12.8b Note the second thrust washer (TS150)

12.11 Note the shaped thrust washer (ES250)

12.12 Remove the circlip

12.13 Replace plastic cover before refitting to swinging arm (ES250)

13.1 The cush drive rubber (TS150)

Chapter 5: Wheels, brakes and tyres

is a retaining flange held by three bolts, which have to be removed first. Removal on the TS models is accomplished by pulling the rubber clear of the sprocket carrier.

3 Examine the rubber for signs of damage or general deterioration. Replace the rubber if there is any doubt about its condition. The usual sign of the cush drive assembly requiring attention is excessive sprocket movement.

14 Speedometer drive

1 The speedometer drive is contained in the rear wheel sprocket carrier. (See Chapter 1, Section 1.12 for the relevant removal procedure, ES250 model).

2 The drive mechanism (all models except ES250), should require little attention except for occasional greasing. Access is obtained by removing the rear wheel sprocket carrier (see Section 12 of this Chapter).

3 The gearbox of the ES250 models can be dismantled by removing the two flange plate screws and lifting off the flange plate. Lift out the gear, noting the thrust washer. The other gear is held in position by the grease nipple, which, when unscrewed, allows it to be removed.

4 Lightly grease and reassemble in the reverse order of dismantling.

14.3a ... lift out gear - note thrust washer

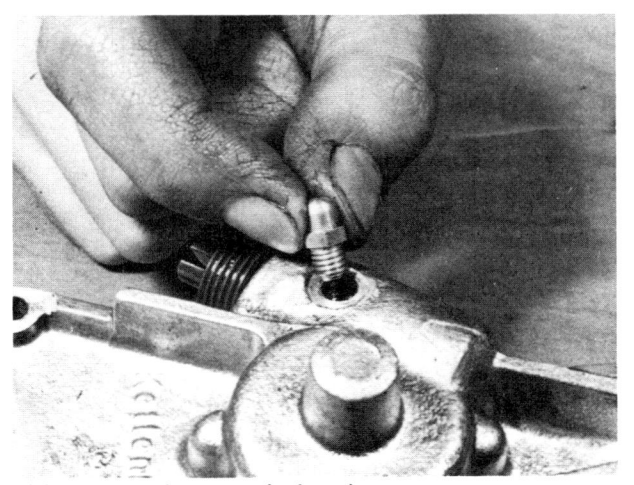

14.1 The speedometer drive gear (TS150)

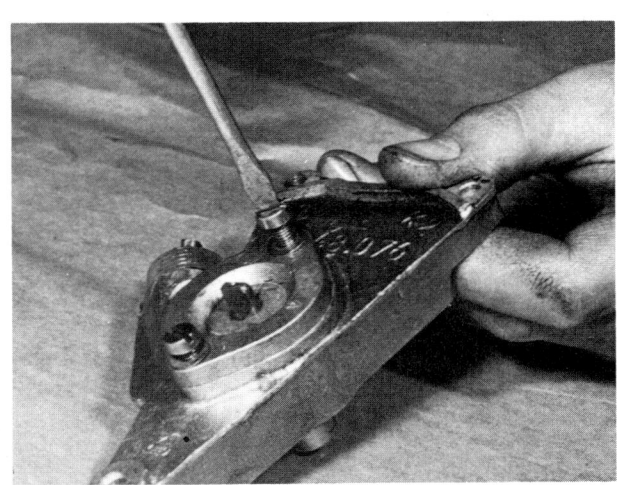

14.3b Unscrew the grease nipple and ...

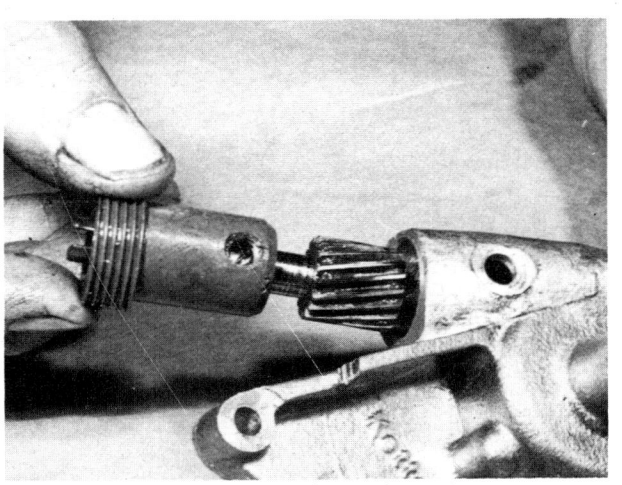

14.3 Remove the two screws and ...

14.3c ... pull out retaining plug and gear (ES250)

15 Rear wheel sprocket

1 The rear wheel sprocket is retained by either 4 bolts, (ES250 models) or 6 bolts (all other models). Access to it is obtained after removing the rear wheel sprocket carrier (see Section 12 of this Chapter).
2 Check the condition of the sprocket teeth. If they are hooked, chipped or badly worn, the sprocket should be renewed.
3 It is bad practice to renew one sprocket on its own. The final drive sprockets should always be renewed as a pair and a new chain fitted, otherwise rapid wear will necessitate even earlier replacement.
4 When replacing the sprocket, do not forget to knock over the tabs of the locking washers.

15.4 Remember to knock over tabs on rear wheel sprocket bolts

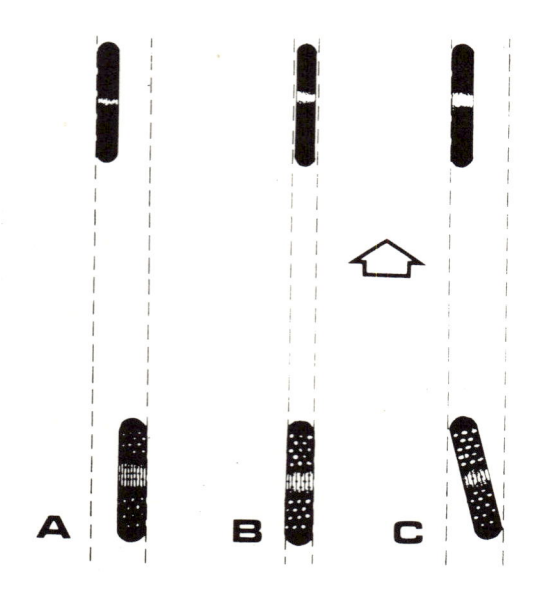

Fig. 5.3 Checking wheel alignment

A and C – Indicate necessity to re-align rear wheel
B – Indicate correct alignment with smaller section front tyre

16 Final drive chain - examination and lubrication

1 The final drive chain is protected by the rubber gaiters and plastic cover over the rear sprocket. Check that the gaiters are not cracked or perished, particularly at the engine end where most flexing occurs.
2 Chain adjustment is correct when there is approximately 20 mm (¾ in.) total play in the middle of the chain run with the machine loaded. Check the chain in several places in case there is a tight spot due to uneven wear. Be careful to feel the actual movement of the chain and not just the rubber gaiter.
3 If the chain is too slack, adjustment is effected by slackening the rear wheel nuts and also the torque arm bolt, then drawing the wheel backwards by means of the cycle-type drawbolt adjusters at the frame ends. Make sure each adjuster is turned an equal amount, so that the rear wheel is kept centrally-disposed within the frame. When the correct adjusting point has been reached, push the wheel hard forward, then tighten the wheel nuts, not forgetting the torque arm bolt, if fitted. Recheck the chain tension and also the wheel alignment, before the final tightening of all nuts.
4 Application of engine oil to the chain from time to time will serve as a satisfactory form of lubrication, but it is preferable to remove the chain every 6,000 miles and clean it in a bath of paraffin before immersing it in a special chain lubricant such as "Linklyfe". This latter type of lubricant achieves better and more lasting penetration of the chain links and rollers and is less likely to be thrown off when the chain is in motion.
5 To check whether the chain needs replacing lay it lengthwise in a straight line and compress it, so that all play is taken up. Anchor one end and then pull on the other, to stretch the chain in the opposite direction. If the chain extends by more than the distance between two adjacent rollers, replacement is advised.
6 When replacing the chain, make sure the spring link is positioned correctly, with the closed end facing the direction of travel. Reconnection is made easier if the ends of the chain are pressed into the teeth of the gearbox sprocket.

17 Tyres - removal and replacement

1 At some time or other the need will arise to remove and replace the tyres, either as the result of a puncture or because a replacement is required to offset wear. To the inexperienced, tyre changing represents a formidable task yet if a few simple rules are observed and the technique learned the whole operation is surprisingly simple.
2 To remove the tyre from either wheel, first detach the wheel from the machine by following the procedure in Sections 2 and 7 of this Chapter, depending on whether the front or the rear wheel is involved. Deflate the tyre by removing the valve insert and when it is fully deflated, push the bead of the tyre away from the wheel rim on both sides so that the bead enters the centre well of the rim. Remove the locking cap and push the tyre valve into the tyre itself.
3 Insert a tyre lever close to the valve and lever the edge of the tyre over the outside of the wheel rim. Very little force should be necessary; if resistance is encountered it is probably due to the fact that the tyre beads have not entered the well of the wheel rim all the way round the tyre.
4 Once the tyre has been edged over the wheel rim, it is easy to work around the wheel rim so that the tyre is completely free on one side. At this stage, the inner tube can be removed.
5 Working from the other side of the wheel, ease the other edge of the tyre over the outside of the wheel rim that is furthest away. Continue to work around the rim until the tyre is free completely from the rim.
6 If a puncture has necessitated the removal of the tyre, re-inflate the inner tube and immerse it in a bowl of water to trace the source of the leak. Mark its position and deflate the tube. Dry the tube and clean the area around the puncture with a petrol-soaked rag. When the surface has dried, apply the rubber

solution and allow this to dry before removing the backing from the patch and applying the patch to the surface.

7 It is best to use a patch of the self-vulcanising type, which will form a very permanent repair. Note that it may be necessary to remove a protective covering from the top surface of the patch, after it has sealed in position. Inner tubes made from synthetic rubber may require a special type of patch and adhesive, if a satisfactory bond is to be achieved.

8 Before replacing the tyre, check the inside to make sure the agent that caused the puncture is not trapped. Check also the outside of the tyre, particularly the tread area, to make sure nothing is trapped that may cause a further puncture.

9 If the inner tube has been patched on a number of past occasions, or if there is a tear or large hole, it is preferable to discard it and fit a replacement. Sudden deflation may cause an accident, particularly if it occurs with the front wheel.

10 To replace the tyre, inflate the inner tube sufficiently for it to assume a circular shape but only just. Then push it into the tyre so that it is enclosed completely. Lay the tyre on the wheel at an angle and insert the valve through the rim tape and the hole in the wheel rim. Attach the locking cap on the first few threads, sufficient to hold the valve captive in its correct location.

11 Starting at the point furthest from the valve, push the tyre bead over the edge of the wheel rim until it is located in the central well. Continue to work around the tyre in this fashion until the whole of one side of the tyre is on the rim. It may be necessary to use a tyre lever during the final stages.

12 Make sure there is no pull on the tyre valve and again commencing with the area furthest from the valve, ease the other bead of the tyre over the edge of the rim. Finish with the area close to the valve, pushing the valve up into the tyre until the locking cap touches the rim. This will ensure the inner tube is not trapped when the last section of the bead is edged over the rim with a tyre lever.

13 Check that the inner tube is not trapped at any point. Re-inflate the inner tube, and check that the tyre is seating correctly around the wheel rim. There should be a thin rib moulded around the wall of the tyre on both sides, which should be equidistant from the wheel rim at all points. If the tyre is unevenly located on the rim, try bouncing the wheel when the tyre is at the recommended pressure. It is probable that one of the beads has not pulled clear of the centre well.

14 Always run the tyres at the recommended pressures and never under or over-inflate. The correct pressures for solo use are 22 psi front and 28 psi rear. If a pillion passenger is carried, increase the rear tyre pressure only to 31 psi.

15 Tyre replacement is aided by dusting the side walls, particularly in the vicinity of the beads, with a liberal coating of french chalk. Washing-up liquid can also be used to good effect, but this has the disadvantage of causing the inner surfaces of the wheel rim to rust.

16 Never replace the inner tube and tyre without the rim tape in position. If this precaution is overlooked there is a good chance of the ends of the spoke nipples chafing the inner tube and causing a crop of punctures.

17 Never fit a tyre that has a damaged tread or side walls. Apart from the legal aspects, there is a very great risk of a blow-out, which can have serious consequences on any two-wheel vehicle.

18 Tyre valves rarely give trouble, but it is always advisable to check whether the valve itself is leaking before removing the tyre. Do not forget to fit the dust cap, which forms an effective second seal.

18 Fault diagnosis :- Wheels, brakes and tyres
Overleaf Page 86

18 Fault diagnosis - wheels, brakes and tyres

Symptom	Cause	Remedy
Handlebars oscillate at low speeds	Buckle or flat in wheel rim, most probably front wheel	Check rim alignment by spinning wheel. Correct by retensioning spokes or having wheel rebuilt on new rim.
	Tyre not straight on rim	Check tyre alignment.
Machine lacks power and accelerates poorly	Brakes binding	Warm brake drums provide best evidence. Readjust brakes.
Brakes grab when applied gently	Ends of brake shoes not chamfered	Chamfer with file.
	Elliptical brake drum	Lightly skim in lathe (specialist attention needed).
Brake pull off sluggish	Brake cam binding in housing	Free and grease.
	Weak brake shoe springs	Replace, if brake springs not displaced.
Harsh transmission	Worn or badly adjusted chains	Adjust or renew as necessary.
	Hooked or badly worn sprockets	Renew as a pair, together with chain.
Steering pulls to one side	Rear wheel misalignment	Adjust rear wheel alignment.

Tyre removal: Deflate inner tube and insert lever in close proximity to tyre valve

Use two levers to work bead over the edge of rim

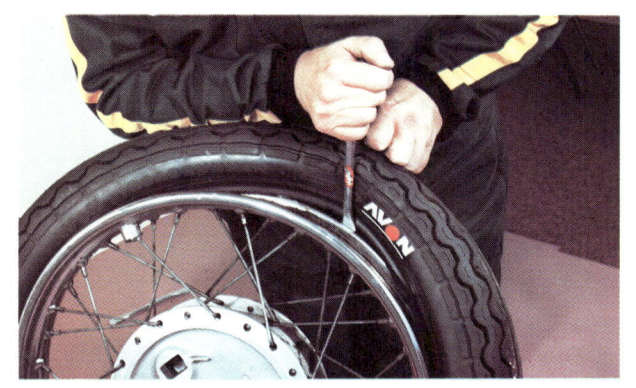

When first bead is clear, remove tyre as shown

Tyre fitting: Inflate inner tube and insert in tyre

Lay tyre on rim and feed valve through hole in rim

Work first bead over rim, using lever in final section

Use similar technique for second bead, finish at tyre valve position

Push valve and tube up into tyre when fitting final section, to avoid trapping

Chapter 6 Electrical equipment

Contents

General description ... 1	Horn - location and adjustment ... 9
Wiring - layout and examination ... 2	Battery - examination and maintenance ... 10
Ignition and light switch ... 3	Charging light ... 11
Fuse - location and replacement ... 4	Regulator - maintenance and setting ... 12
Headlamp - replacing bulbs and adjusting beam height ... 5	Dynamo - checking ... 13
Rear lamp and stop lamp - replacing bulbs ... 6	Dynamo - carbon brushes and commutator ... 14
Direction indicators - replacing bulbs ... 7	Fault diagnosis - electrical system ... 15
Stop lamp switch - adjustment ... 8	

Specifications

Lighting ... 6 volt system, all models

Bulb ratings
Headlight ...	45/40W (TS250 35/35W)
Sidelight ...	4W (ES150 2W)
Rear light ...	5W
Stop light ...	18W (TS150 21W)
Indicator ...	18W (TS150 21W)
Charging control light ...	1.2W
Neutral light ...	1.2W
Speedometer ...	1.2W

Battery
Rating ... 6 volt 12 amp/hrs.

Dynamo
Output continuous ...	6V 60W
Output intermittent ...	6V 90W

1 General description

The MZ range of motorcycles use a crankshaft mounted dynamo to supply the necessary electrical current. The charging rate and voltage regulation is achieved by an adjustable resistor coil and regulator box. A 6 volt negative earth system is used. Dynamo switching facilities are provided for emergency starting when the battery is fully discharged.

2 Wiring - layout and examination

1 The wiring harness is colour-coded and will correspond with the accompanying wiring diagrams.
2 Visual inspection will show whether any breaks or frayed outer coverings are giving rise to short circuits. Another source of trouble may be the snap connectors, particularly where the connector has not been pushed home fully in the outer casing.
3 Intermittent short circuits can often be traced to a chafed wire that passes through or close to a metal component, such as a frame member. Avoid tight bends in the wire or situations where the wire can become trapped or stretched between casings.

3 Ignition and light switch

1 A combined ignition and light switch is fitted in the top of the headlamp unit. If the switch malfunctions it should be renewed rather than risk sudden failure of the ignition or the lights as the result of a bad or intermittent contact.
2 On no account oil the switch since this will foul the contacts and thereby initiate failure.

4 Fuse - location and replacement

1 Two 15 amp fuses are located behind the left-hand side cover, or to the rear of the air filter in the case of the TS250 model. A separate 8 amp fuse in a plastic holder, located in the headlight shell, is fitted for the four direction indicator lamps, a 4 amp fuse being used if the direction indicating system is of the two lamp variety.
2 If a fuse blows the electrical circuit should be checked for a fault before replacing it with another.
3 Always carry spare fuses. These will get you home in an emergency, provided the reason for the original failure has been traced and remedied. Never use a fuse of a higher rating or its

Chapter 6: Electrical system

protective function will be lost.

4 When a fuse blows whilst the machine is running and no spare fuse is available, a get you home remedy is to remove the blown fuse and to wrap it in silver paper. This will restore electrical continuity by bridging the broken wire within the fuse. This expedient should **never** be used if there is evidence of a short circuit or other major electrical fault, otherwise more serious damage will be caused. Replace the temporary fuse at the earliest possible opportunity to restore full circuit protection.

5 Headlamp - replacing bulbs and adjusting beam height

1 On TS models remove the headlamp rim by undoing the rim screw and pulling the rim off complete with reflector. On ES models it is necessary to remove the four screws and pull out the surround. The headlamp unit is retained by two clips.

2 The headlamp and pilot light bulbs are retained in the reflector by a clip.

3 Beam height on the ES models is adjusted by the two screws positioned at 10 o'clock and 4 o'clock as shown in the accompanying photograph. On the TS model the beam height is adjusted by slackening the two headlamp shell retaining bolts and tilting the headlamp either upwards or downwards. Adjustments should always be made with the rider normally seated.

4 UK lighting regulations stipulate that the lighting system must be arranged so that the light will not dazzle a person standing in the same horizontal plane as the vehicle at a distance greater than 25 yards from the lamp, whose eye level is not less than 3 feet 6 inches above that plane. It is easy to approximate this setting by placing the machine 25 yards away from a wall, on a level road, and setting the beam height so that it is concentrated at the same height as the distance from the centre of the headlamp to the ground. The rider must be seated normally during this operation and also the pillion passenger, if one is carried regularly.

6 Rear lamp and stop lamp - replacing bulbs

1 Separate bulbs are fitted for the rear and stop lamps. Access to the bulbs is obtained by removing the screws that retain the plastic lens. Do not forget to replace the rubber ring.

7 Direction indicators - replacing bulbs

1 On early models only, two direction indicators were fitted which use two 18W festoon bulbs. Later models are fitted with a four lamp system utilising 21W bayonet fitting bulbs.

2 Access to each bulb is obtained by removing the two screws and pulling off the lens cover. When replacing a bulb make sure it is of the correct wattage otherwise the flashing rate will be affected.

8 Stop lamp switch - adjustment

1 The stop lamp switch is integral with the rear brake plate. For adjustment refer to Chapter 5, Section 11.

9 Horn - location and adjustment

1 The horn is fitted either below the front of the tank or on the bottom yoke of the front forks, according to the model designation.

2 If the horn does not function, first check the horn button and wiring. The horn can be adjusted by turning the slotted screw at the rear until the desired tone and volume is attained.

3 Note that a multi-leaf bracket is used to fit the horn. This is used to prevent the bracket from fracturing as the result of vibration.

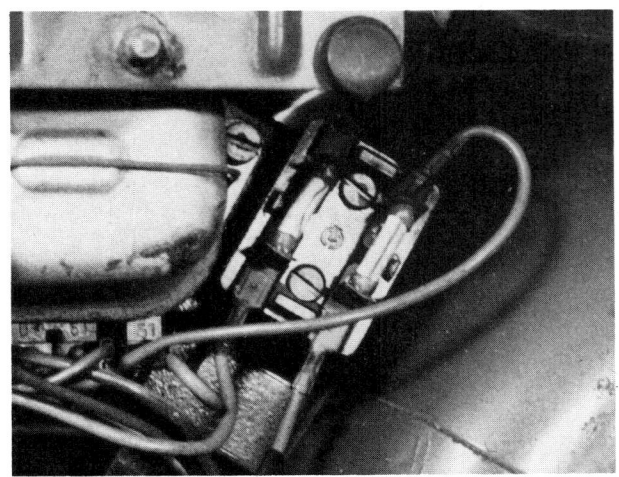

4.1 The two main fuses

5.1 Undo the retaining screw (TS150)

5.1a Remove the four screws and pull out headlamp surround (ES250)

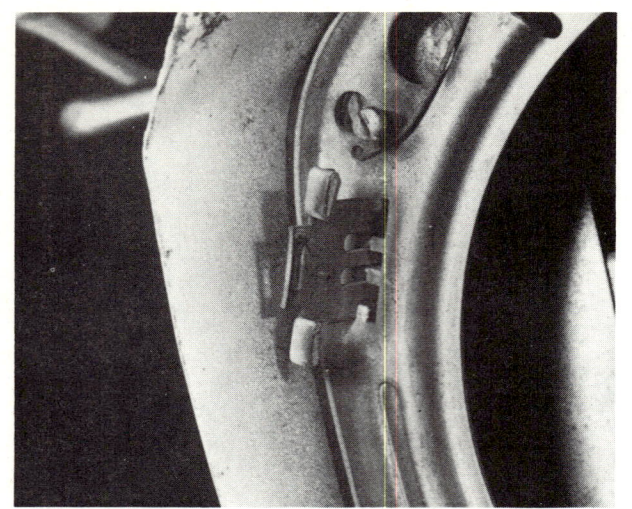

5.1b The headlamp unit is held by two clips (ES250)

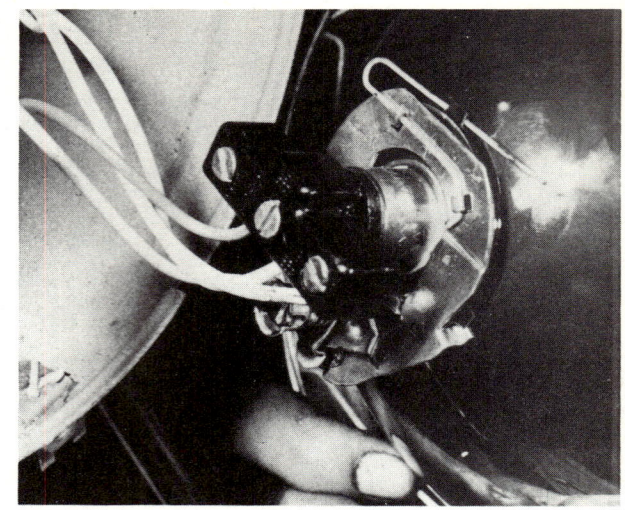

5.2 Lift wire clip to remove headlamp bulbs

5.3 The headlamp beam adjusting screws (ES250)

6.1 Separate festoon bulbs used for rear and stop lamps (ES250)

6.1a Replace the rubber sealing ring

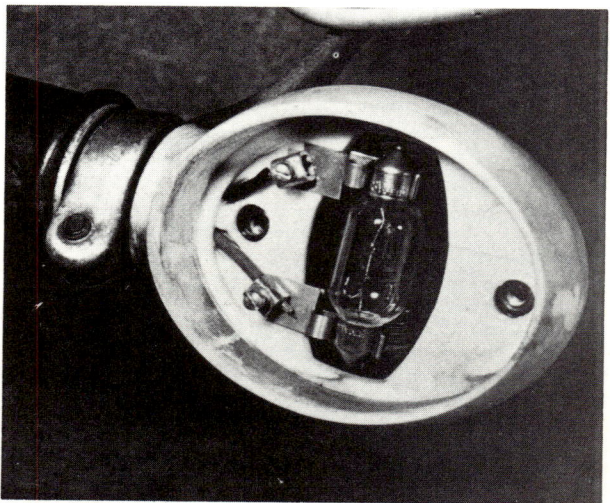

7.2 The indicator bulb of the two lamp system

Chapter 6: Electrical system

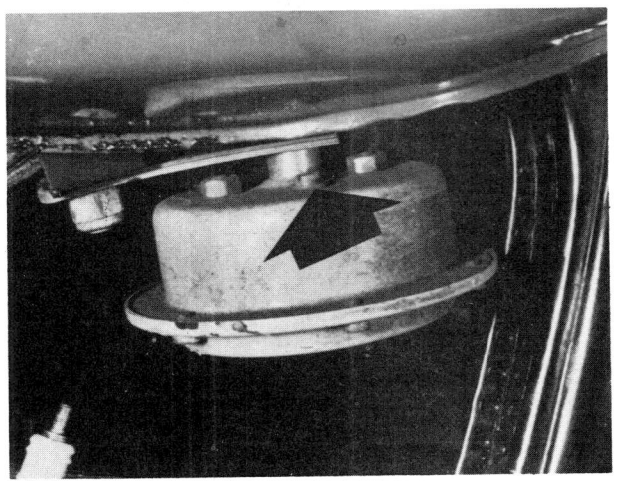

9.2 Turn screw to adjust horn tone and volume

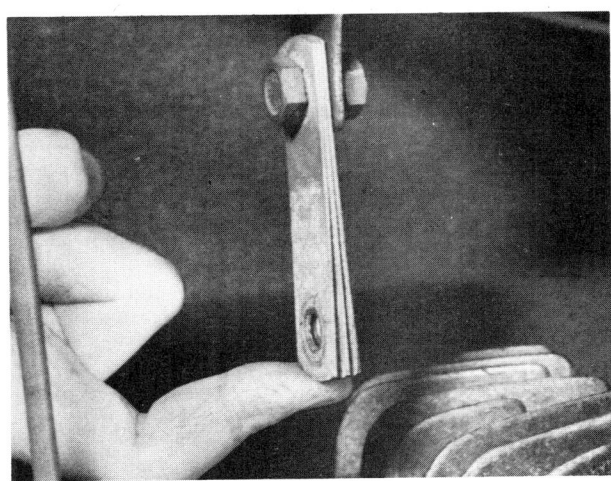

9.3 To prevent fracture anti-vibration horn bracket is fitted

10 Battery - examination and maintenance

1 The electrolyte level of the battery should be maintained between the upper and lower limits marked on the case by topping-up with distilled water (unless spillage has occurred when it should be topped-up with acid of the correct specific gravity). If when the battery is in a fully charged condition, (corresponding to approximately 6.6 volts) and the specific gravity lies much below 1.26 - 1.28 at 20°C, it should be replaced by fresh sulphuric acid of the correct specific gravity (1.26 - 1.28 at 20°C).

2 If the machine has not been used for some time, to prevent deterioration, the battery should be recharged every six weeks or so. If the battery is left in a discharged condition for any length of time the plates will sulphate and render it inoperative.

3 A normal charging rate of 1 amp should be used when charging the battery off the machine.

4 When reconnecting the battery, make sure that it is connected the correct way round ie; negative earth. Damage to the dynamo and regulator box will result if the connections are inadvertently transposed.

11 Charging light

1 The charging light serves also as the direction indicator warning light. If the light does not function normally, check the following points for possible faults. If the light fails to go out at high rpm, either the terminal D+ on the regulator, wire 61 (see wiring diagram), or the field coil of the dynamo has shorted to earth, or the regulator is failing to function.

If, with the ignition on, but the engine not running, the bulb fails to light, the cause could be one of the following:

a) *Battery discharged.*
b) *Fuse blown.*
c) *The wire from 30 (see wiring diagram) to the ignition switch, or the wire 31 from the battery, is broken.*
d) *The wire from D+ on the dynamo to the regulator, or wire 61 from the regulator to the ignition switch and charging light is broken.*
e) *Bulb blown.*
f) *Regulator cut-out defective.*

12 Regulator - maintenance and setting

1 The adjustable resistor coil and regulator maintain the current charging of the battery and supply of current to the electrical system of the motorcycle.

2 The regulator should require little maintenance, except for occasional cleaning of the contacts. If, for any reason, it is required to reset the regulator, use the settings given in Fig. 6.1. These settings should give the following results:

Make voltage	6.5 - 6.9V
Break voltage	5.4 - 6.2V
Rated load voltage	6.2 - 6.8V
(at 1800 - 2200 rpm)	

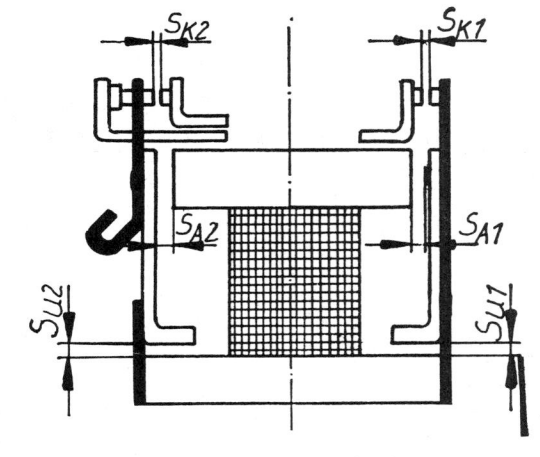

Fig. 6.1 Regulator: mechanical settings

S_{K1} = 0.4 mm
S_{K2} = 0.3 to 0.4 mm
S_{A1} = 1.0 mm
S_{A2} = 0.9 to 1.1 mm
S_{U1} = 0.5 mm
S_{U2} = 0.5 mm

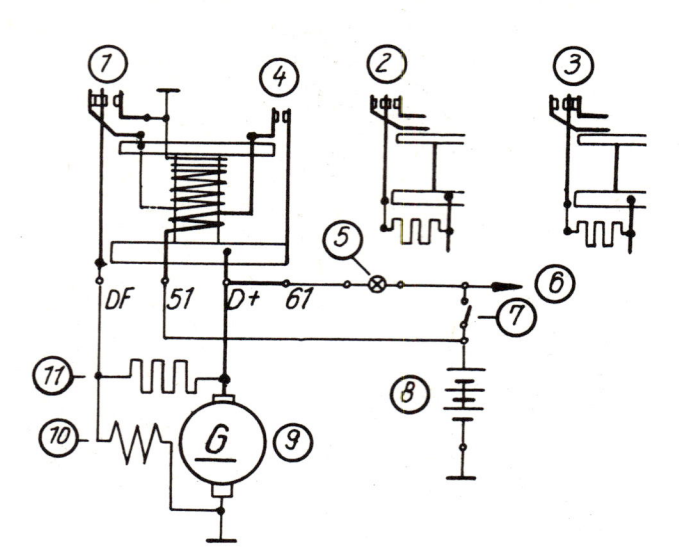

Chapter 6: Electrical system

Fig. 6.2 Circuit diagram of regulator (three control positions)

1 Lower position
2 Suspended position
3 Upper position
4 Reverse-current switch
5 Charging-control light
6 Ignition, terminal 15
7 Ignition switch
8 Battery 6 V, 12 Ah
9 Dynamo 6 V, 60 W
10 Field coil 1.7 to 2.1
11 Adjustable resistor 4.5

12.1 The adjustable resistor coil

12.1a Lift clip and remove cover to expose regulator contacts

14.1 Pull out the brush springs followed by ...

13 Dynamo - checking

1 If the dynamo is suspected to be faulty it is possible to check the wiring if a suitable multi-meter is available. If not, the unit will have to be returned to an MZ dealer or an auto electrical repair specialist for checking.
2 Check the armature for shorts by connecting the meter between ground (the armature laminations) and each of the commutator segments. There should be no reading on the meter.
3 It is not possible to check the armature for shorted windings with a multi-meter.
4 Disconnect the field coil from ground and the resistor coil. There should be no reading between ground and the DF terminal. If a short is found each coil will have to be tested individually. If this test is satisfactory, check the resistance of the field coil by connecting the meter across the negative and positive side of the coil. A reading of 1.7 - 2.1 ohms should be obtained. If less than 1.7 ohms, some turns of the coil are shorted, and if no reading is obtained the coil is open circuit and defective.

14 Dynamo - carbon brushes and commutator

1 The two carbon brushes should be checked every 3,000 miles. They are removed by undoing their connecting leads and pulling them out from their holders.
2 Check that the brushes are free to move in their holders and the braided copper is in good condition. Renew the brushes if they are shorter than 9 mm.
3 Examine the commutator and clean it with a little metal polish if it is very dirty. Be careful to remove all polish afterwards. If the commutator is ridged it should be skimmed in a lathe and the mica undercut by 0.2 - 0.4 mm with a maximum width of 0.7 mm.

Chapter 6: Electrical system

14.1a ... the brushes

14.3 Examine commutator for scoring

15 Fault diagnosis - electrical system

Symptom	Cause	Remedy
Complete electrical failure	Short circuit	Check wiring and electrical components for short circuit and eliminate it.
	Isolated battery	Check battery connections, also whether connections show signs of corrosion.
Dim lights, horn inoperative	Discharge battery	Recharge battery with battery charger and check whether dynamo is giving correct output (electrical specialist).
Constantly 'blowing' bulbs	Vibration, poor earth connection	Check whether bulb holders are secured correctly. Check earth return or connections to frame.

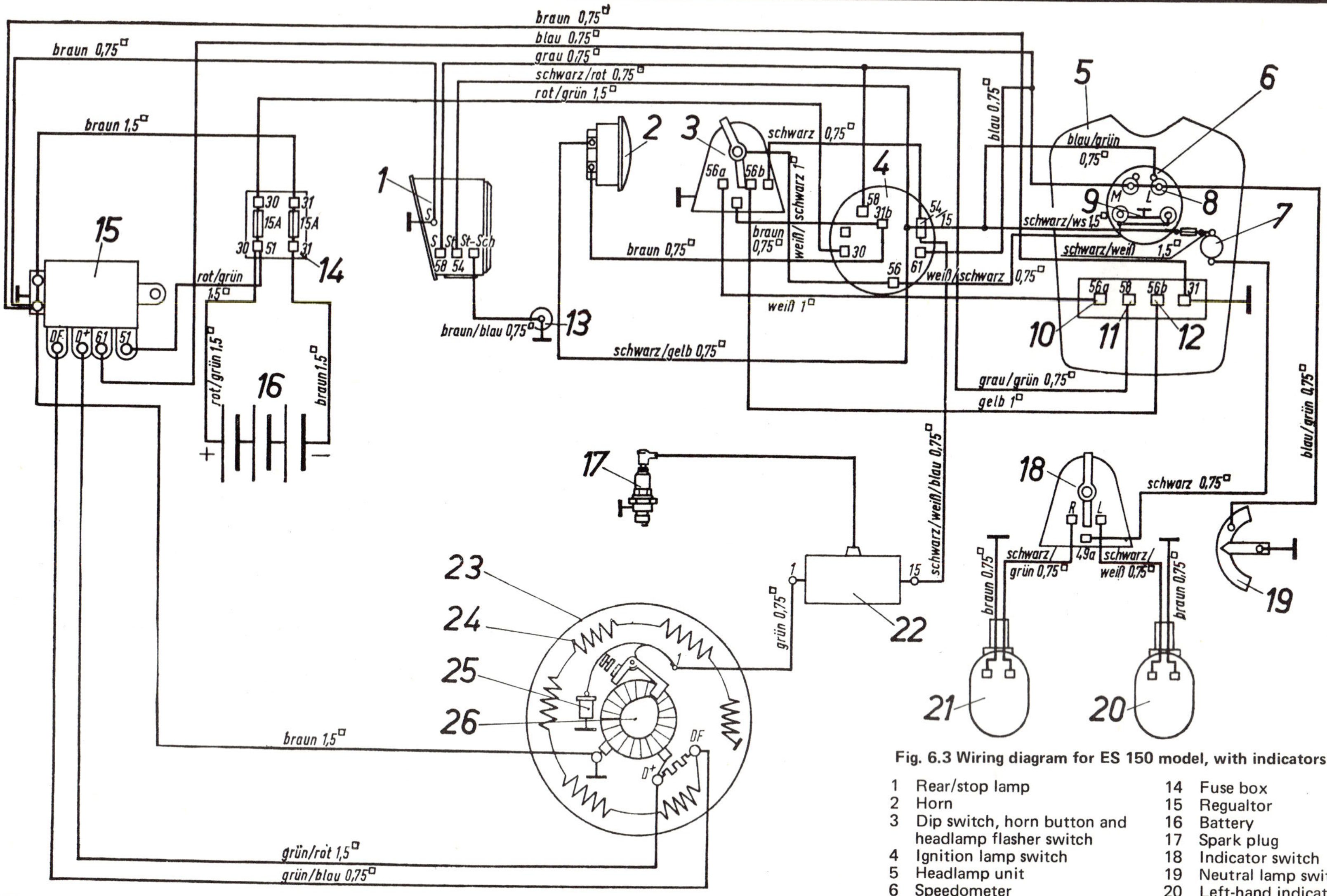

94

Fig. 6.3 Wiring diagram for ES 150 model, with indicators

1 Rear/stop lamp
2 Horn
3 Dip switch, horn button and headlamp flasher switch
4 Ignition lamp switch
5 Headlamp unit
6 Speedometer
7 Flasher unit
8 Control lamps
9 Speedometer lamp
10 Main beam
11 Parking lamp
12 Dip beam
13 Stop lamp switch
14 Fuse box
15 Regualtor
16 Battery
17 Spark plug
18 Indicator switch
19 Neutral lamp switch
20 Left-hand indicator
21 Right-hand indicator
22 Ignition coil
23 Dynamo
24 Dynamo field coil
25 Condenser
26 Contact breaker cam

Colours

braun	brown	rot	red
blau	blue	grün	green
grau	grey	weiß	white
scwarz	black		

All figures after colour codes refer to the cross section (mm²) of the wires

Fig. 6.4 Wiring diagram for TS150 model, without indicators

1 Headlamp unit
  a. Parking light
  b. Main beam
  c. Dip beam
  d. Ignition lamp switch
  f. Speedometer lamp
  g. Charging control lamp
2 Handlebar control switch
  a. Horn button
  b. Dip switch
  c. Headlamp flasher
3 Horn
4 Dynamo
  a. Contact breaker
5 Ignition coil
6 Spark plug
7 Battery
8 Neutral lamp switch
  h. Neutral lamp
9 Fuse box
10 Regulator
11 Rear lamp unit
  a. Stop lamp
  b. Rear lamp
12 Stop lamp switch

Colour code

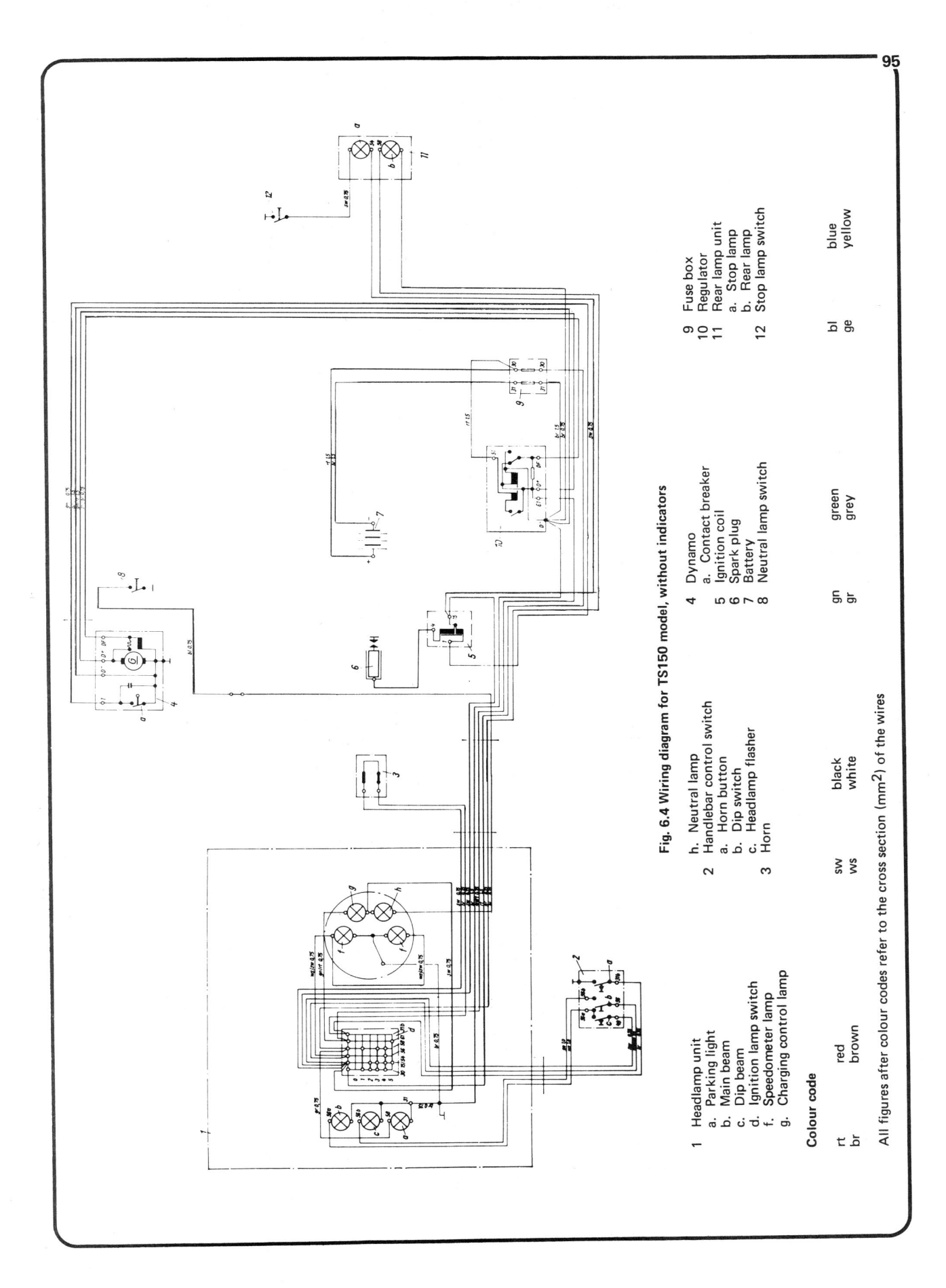

rt	red	sw	black	gn	green	bl	blue
br	brown	ws	white	gr	grey	ge	yellow

All figures after colour codes refer to the cross section (mm^2) of the wires

Fig. 6.5 Wiring diagram for TS150 model, with indicators

1 Headlamp unit
 a. Parking lamp
 b. Main beam
 c. Dip beam
 d. Ignition lamp switch
 e. Flasher unit
 f. Speedometer lamp
 g. Charging control lamp
 h. Neutral lamp
 i. Terminal strip
2 Indicator switch
3 Handlebar control switch
 a. Horn button
 b. Dip switch
 c. Headlamp flasher
4 Horn
5 Dynamo
6 Ignition coil
7 Spark plug
8 Battery
9 Neutral lamp switch
10 Fuse box
11 Regulator
12 Terminal strip
 a. Contact breaker
13 Rear lamp unit
 a. Stop lamp
 b. Rear lamp
14 Stop lamp switch
15 Left-hand front indicator
16 Right-hand front indicator
17 Left-hand rear indicator
18 Right-hand rear indicator

Colour code

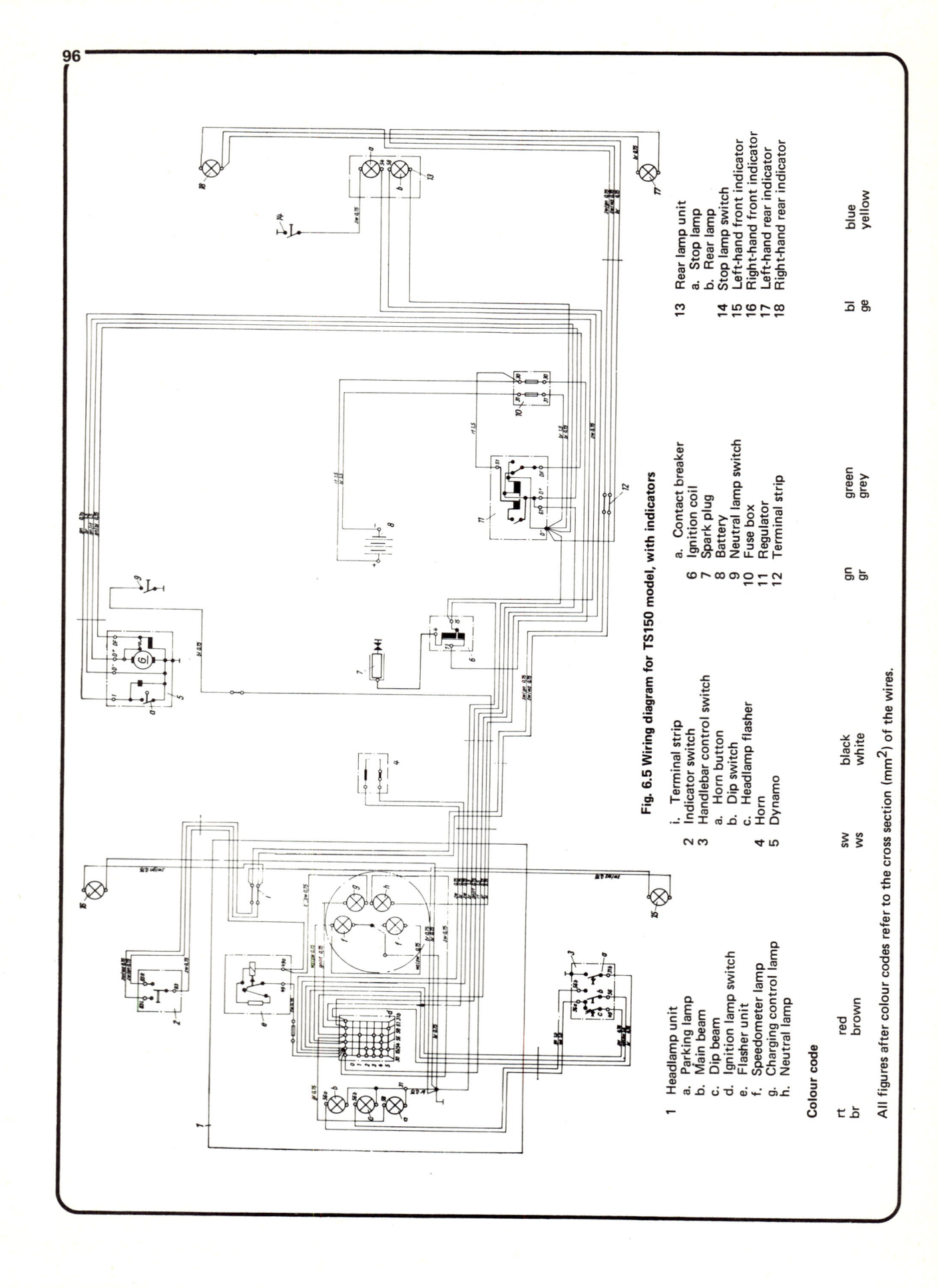

| rt | red | sw | black | gn | green | bl | blue |
| br | brown | ws | white | gr | grey | ge | yellow |

All figures after colour codes refer to the cross section (mm^2) of the wires.

Fig. 6.6 Wiring diagrams for TS250 model, with indicators

1 Headlamp unit
  a. Parking lamp
  b. Main beam
  c. Dip beam
  d. Ignition lamp switch
  g. Speedometer lamp
  h. Charging control lamp
  i. Neutral lamp
2 Indicator lamp switch
3 Handlebar control switch
  a. Horn button
  b. Dip switch
  c. Headlamp flasher
4 Horn
5 Dynamo
6 a. Contact breaker
7 Ignition coil
   Spark plug
8 Battery
9 Neutral lamp switch
10 Fuse box
11 Regualtor
12 Connecting block
13 Rear lamp unit
  a. Stop lamp
  b. Rear lamp
14 Stop lamp switch
15 Left-hand front indicator
16 Right-hand front indicator
17 Left-hand rear indicator
18 Right-hand rear indicator

Colour code

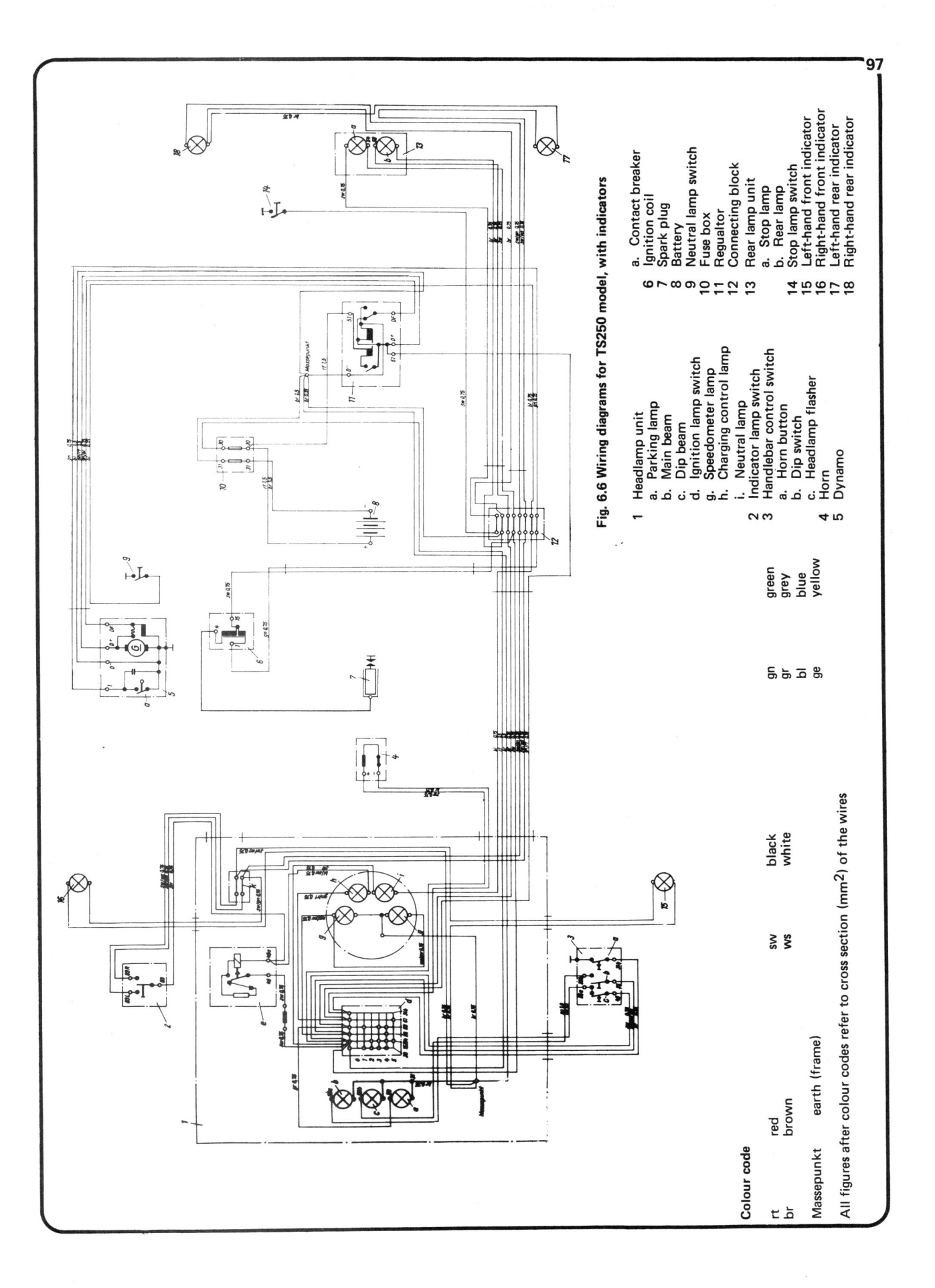

rt red   sw black   gn green
br brown   ws white   gr grey
                                                bl blue
Massepunkt earth (frame)   ge yellow

All figures after colour codes refer to cross section (mm²) of the wires

Fig. 6.7 Wiring diagram for TS250 model, without indicators

1 Headlamp unit
  a. Parking lamp
  b. Main beam
  c. Dip beam
  d. Ignition lamp switch
  g. Speedometer lamp
  h. Charging control lamp
2 Indicator lamp switch
3 Handlebar control switch
  a. Horn button
  b. Dip switch
  c. Headlamp flasher
4 Horn
i. Neutral lamp
5 Dynamo
  a. Contact breaker
6 Ignition coil
7 Spark plug
8 Battery
9 Neutral lamp switch
10 Fuse box
11 Regulator
12 Connecting block
13 Rear lamp unit
  a. Stop lamp
  b. Rear lamp
14 Stop lamp switch

Colour codes

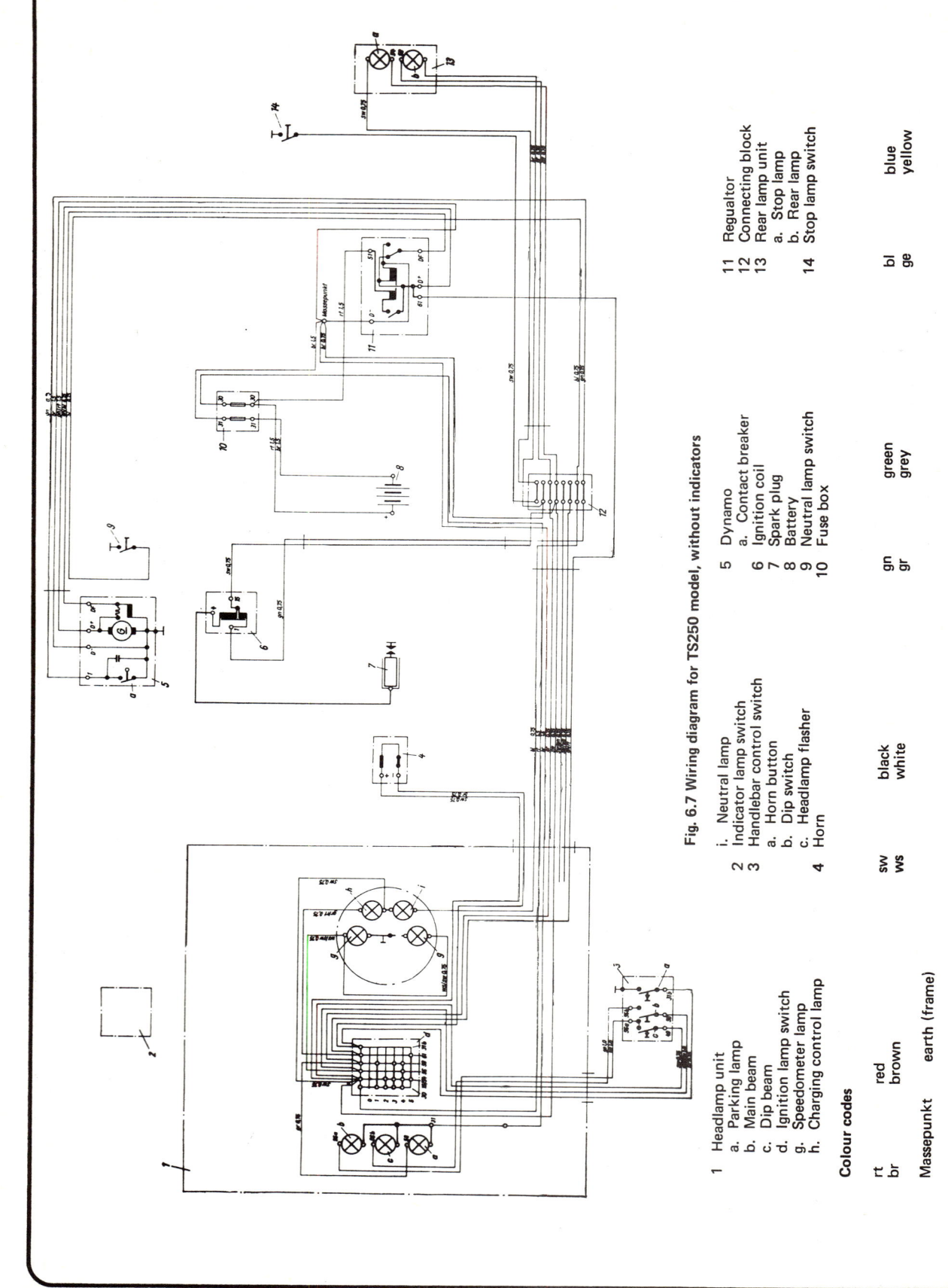

rt	red	gn	green	bl	blue
br	brown	gr	grey	ge	yellow
sw	black				
ws	white				

Massepunkt   earth (frame)

All figures after colour codes refer to cross section (mm²) of the wires

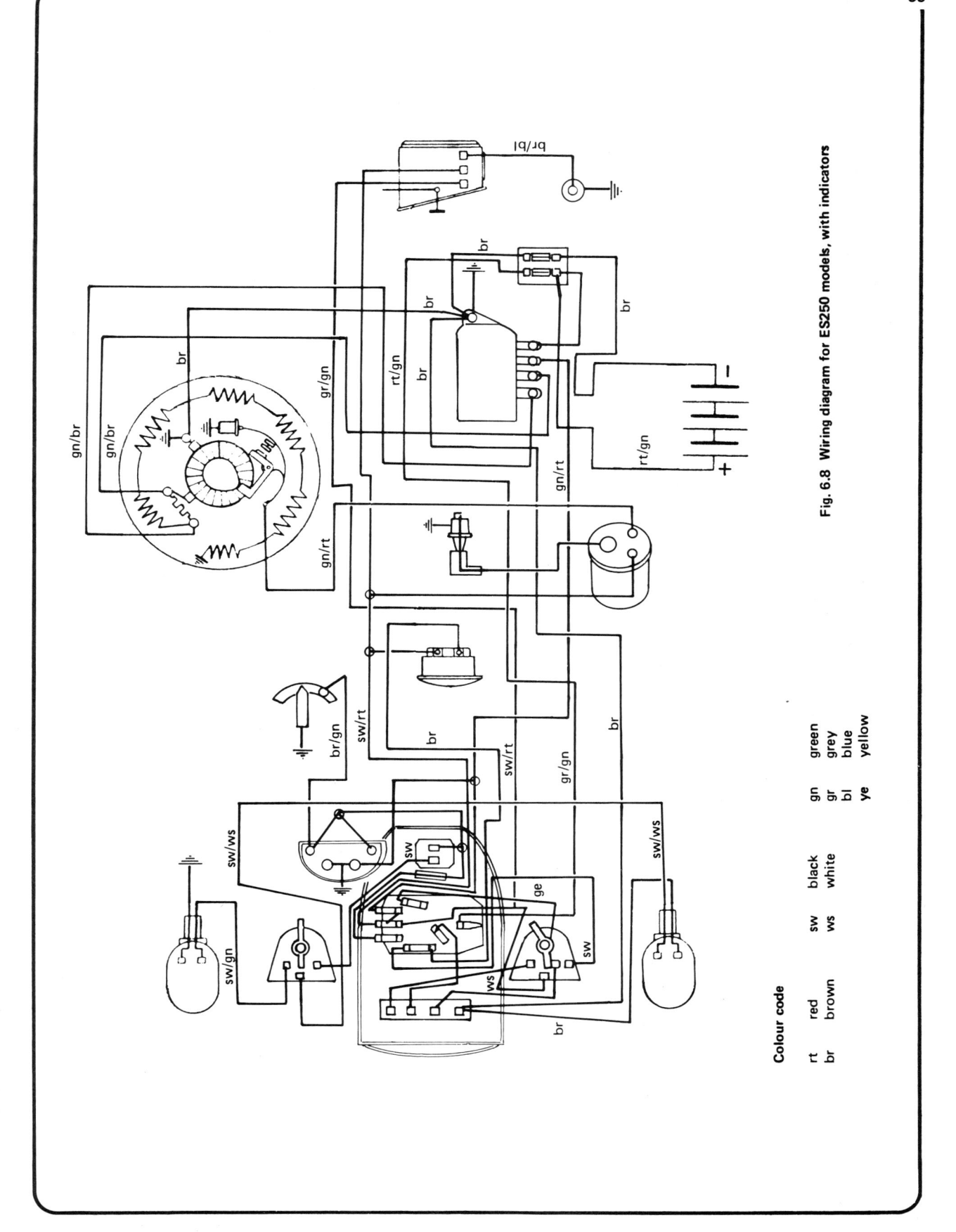

Fig. 6.8 Wiring diagram for ES250 models, with indicators

Colour code

rt	red	sw	black	gn	green
br	brown	ws	white	gr	grey
				bl	blue
				ye	yellow

Right - hand view of 1979 MZ 250/1

Chapter 7 The TS 250/1 model

Contents

TS 250/1 model-comparison with TS 250 ... 1	Dismantling, removing and renovating the fork legs ... 6
Removal of the engine unit from the frame ... 2	Removal and replacement of the headlamp bulb ... 7
The five-speed gearbox ... 3	Removal and replacement of the tail/stop lamp bulbs ... 8
Kickstart ... 4	Removal and replacement of the flashing
Front forks ... 5	indicator bulbs ... 9

Dimensions and weight

Length ...	2075 mm 81.69 ins
Width (+ mirror and low handlebar) ...	730 mm 28.74 ins
Width (+ mirror and high handlebar) ...	865 mm 34.06 ins
Height (+ mirror and low handlebar) ...	1136 mm 44.72 ins
Height (+ mirror and high handlebar) ...	1195 mm 47.05 ins
Dry weight ...	130 kg 286.06 lbs

Quick glance maintenance

Petrol:oil ratio ...	50:1
Fuel tank capacity ...	17.5 Litres (3.85 imp galls)
Gearbox oil capacity ...	900 cc gear oil
Contact breaker gap ...	0.3 mm
Spark plug ...	NGK B77HC
Spark plug gap ...	0.024 in (0.6 mm)
Fork oil capacity ...	230 cc each leg
Tyre pressures:	
Front ...	22 lbs/in^2
Rear solo ...	29 lbs/in^2
Rear with pillion passenger ...	31 lbs/in^2

Chapter 7: The TS250/1 model

Specifications

Engine	single cylinder two-stroke
Bore	69 mm
Stroke	65 mm
Displacement	244 cc
Compression ratio	9.5 - 10:1
Power output	21 SAE-PS at 5,200-5,500 rpm
Max. torque	2.6 kgf m at 4,600-5,200 rpm
Gearbox	5-speed
Ratios:	
First	3.0 : 1
Second	1.87 : 1
Third	1.33 : 1
Fourth	1.05 : 1
Top	0.87 : 1
Final drive reduction	20:47 teeth = 1:2.35 solo
Gearbox/rear wheel sprocket (for sidecar use)	16:47 teeth = 1 :2.92
Clutch	wet multi-plate disc
Carburettor	
Type	BVF 30 N 2-4
Main jet	135
Needle jet	70
Air adjusting screw	1 turn out
Ignition	battery and coil
Battery	6V 12Ah
Dynamo	dc dynamo 6V60/90W output
Spark plug	NGK B77HC
Spark plug gap	0.024 in (0.6 mm)
Frame	Parallel tubular frame
Front forks	telescopic
Front fork travel	185 mm
Front fork capacity	230 cc each leg
Oil level	280 mm
Rear suspension	swinging arm
Rear suspension travel	105 mm
Tyres	
Front tyre	2.75 18 inch
Rear tyre	2.50 16 inch
Front tyre pressure	22 lbs/in^2
Rear tyre pressure	solo 29 lbs/in^2
	with pillion 31 lbs/in^2

1 TS250/1 model-comparison with the TS250

1 The MZ TS250/1 has been developed from the earlier TS250 model with particular reference to the drive mechanism. In order to provide greater flexibility, a 5-speed gearbox has been incorporated in the specification of this new model, which has necessitated a redesigned gear selector mechanism. Other improvements have been incorporated at the same time, such as the introduction of better main bearings with an improved sealing arrangement, a redesigned cylinder head with horizontal finning, and rubber noise damping strips between the cylinder fins. An improved clutch operating mechanism is also employed on the new TS250/1 model. These changes do not significantly affect the strip down or rebuilding procedures detailed in the earlier chapters of this manual.

2 With regard to the cycle parts of the TS250/1, a new design of telescopic front forks is used, the new forks giving a total of 185 mm fork travel.

3 The braking performance of the new model has been improved by the use of cast iron brake drums in the original wheels. In most other respects the specification is similar to that of the original TS250 model.

Chapter 7: The TS250/1 model

2 Removal of the engine unit from the frame

1 The TS250/1 engine unit has an engine damper which links the cylinder head to the frame. Before the engine unit can be removed, this must be detached from the unit. It will also be necessary to detach the clutch cable before any start can be made to remove the unit from the frame. This can be achieved by unscrewing the sleeve and pushing the cable sideways (see photograph 2.1). The cable can then be unclipped and drawn out. This revised method of removing the clutch cable from the engine unit is necessary as a new clutch operating mechanism is used.

2 Undo the two bolts at either side of the engine damper to release it from the engine unit. Then undo the remaining engine bolts underneath the engine unit upon which the engine hinges. It is a good idea to have a friend at hand who can assist with the engine removal when it is being taken out of the frame (and also when replacing the engine in the frame). To replace the engine in the frame reverse the removal procedure.

3 The five-speed gearbox

1 The use of a five-speed gearbox has necessitated a certain amount of redesign of the gear selector mechanism. The accompanying illustrations show the general layout.

2 To remove the gear cluster it is necessary to withdraw both the mainshaft and the layshaft assembly together with the gear selector drum. This may be carried out firstly by removing the gearchange shaft and arm. Push the gearchange pawl towards the gearchange shaft, which will enable the shaft to be disengaged from the selector drum. The shaft and arm may then be withdrawn easily.

3 Take the plain washer off the selector fork spindle, then remove the detent bolt from the casing. Take care not to lose the spring and ball bearing within it. The shafts and drum may then be withdrawn from the casing.

4 Should it be necessary to dismantle the individual gearshafts, this may easily be carried out by removing the relevant circlips and washers, labelling each component carefully and noting their positions, to enable quick and easy reassembly.

5 The gearbox may be reassembled by reversing the dismantling procedure. Reference to the accompanying photographs will aid the reassembly of the gears in their correct sequence. When refitting the gear cluster to the crankcase, the gear selector drum should be offered up at the same time with the selector forks in their correct locations. It should then be easy to refit them in this built up form.

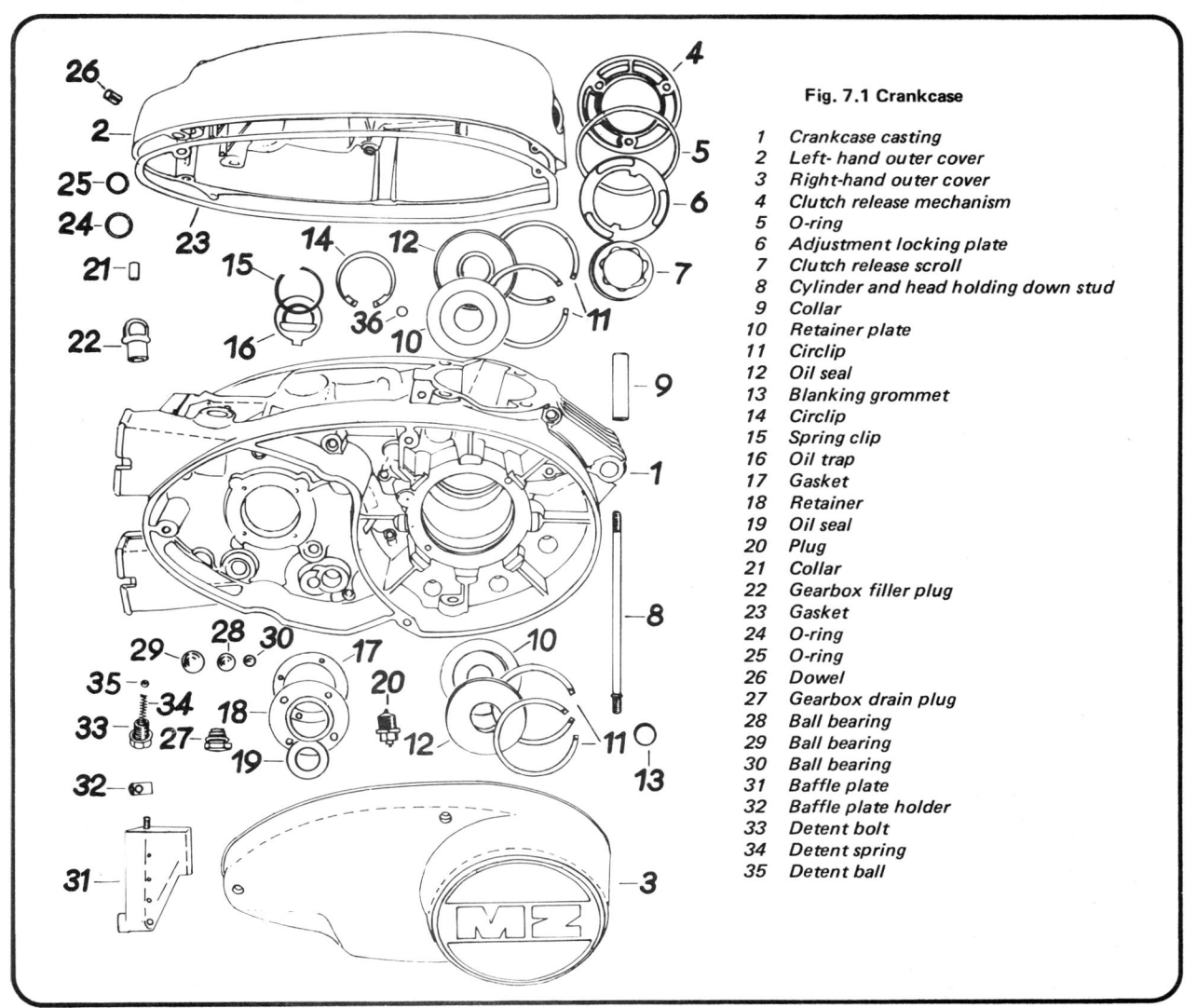

Fig. 7.1 Crankcase

1 Crankcase casting
2 Left-hand outer cover
3 Right-hand outer cover
4 Clutch release mechanism
5 O-ring
6 Adjustment locking plate
7 Clutch release scroll
8 Cylinder and head holding down stud
9 Collar
10 Retainer plate
11 Circlip
12 Oil seal
13 Blanking grommet
14 Circlip
15 Spring clip
16 Oil trap
17 Gasket
18 Retainer
19 Oil seal
20 Plug
21 Collar
22 Gearbox filler plug
23 Gasket
24 O-ring
25 O-ring
26 Dowel
27 Gearbox drain plug
28 Ball bearing
29 Ball bearing
30 Ball bearing
31 Baffle plate
32 Baffle plate holder
33 Detent bolt
34 Detent spring
35 Detent ball

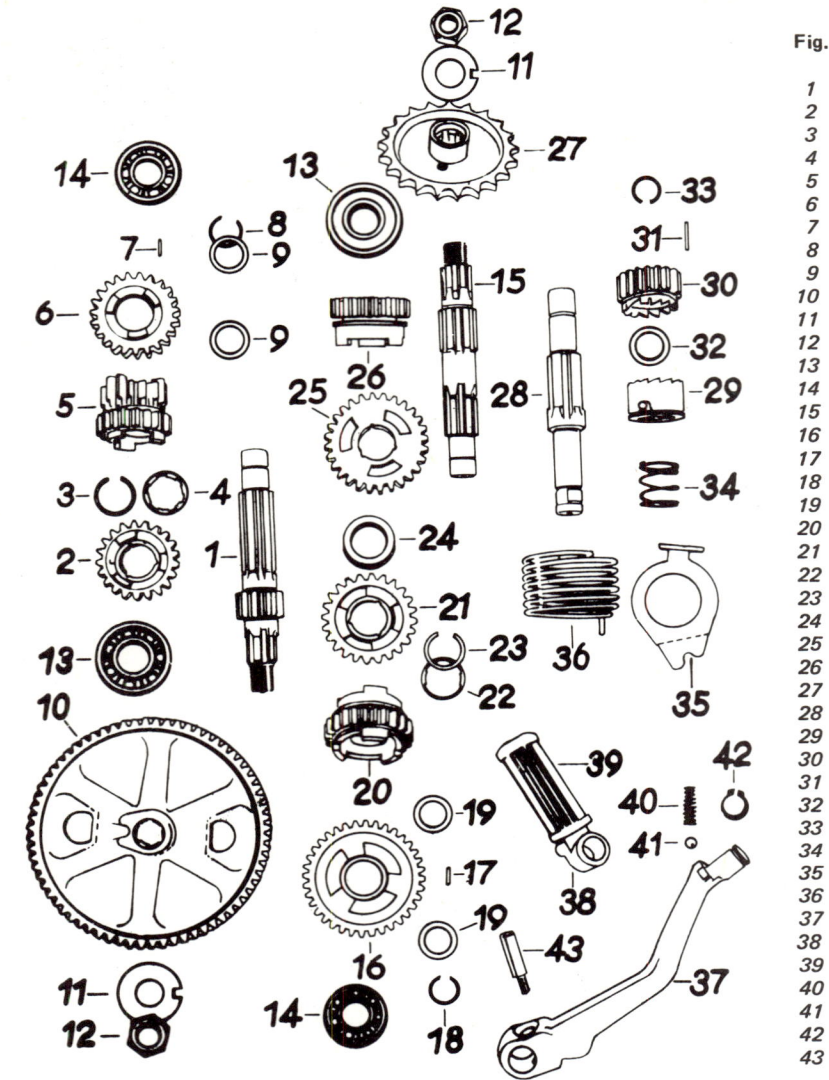

Fig. 7.2 Gearbox and kickstart components

1 Mainshaft
2 Mainshaft 4th gear pinion
3 Circlip
4 Thrust washer
5 Mainshaft 2nd and 3rd gear pinion
6 Mainshaft 5th gear pinion
7 Needle roller - 24 off
8 Circlip
9 Thrust washer - 2 off
10 Primary driven gear
11 Locking washer
12 Mainshaft nut
13 Mainshaft bearing
14 Mainshaft bearing
15 Layshaft
16 Layshaft 1st gear pinion
17 Needle roller - 24 off
18 Circlip
19 Thrust washer - 2 off
20 Layshaft 4th gear pinion
21 Layshaft 3rd gear pinion
22 Thrust washer
23 Spring clip
24 Spacer
25 Layshaft 2nd gear pinion
26 Layshaft 5th gear pinion
27 Gearbox sprocket
28 Kickstart shaft
29 Kickstart ratchet
30 Kickstart pinion
31 Needle roller - 24 off
32 Thrust washer
33 Circlip
34 Ratchet spring
35 Stop plate
36 Kickstart return spring
37 Kickstart lever
38 Kickstart foot end
39 Kickstart end cover
40 Spring
41 Ball
42 Circlip
43 Cotter pin

2.1 Detaching the clutch cable

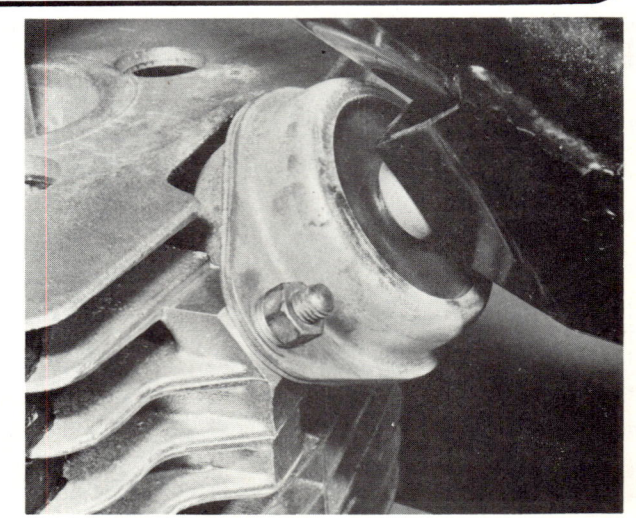

2.2a Engine damper in positon

2.2b Engine damper with engine removed

3.2 Push the gearchange pawl towards the gearchange shaft to disengage it from the selector drum

3.3 Remove the detent bolt

3.5a Reassemble the gear cluster starting with the layshaft 2nd gear pinion

3.5b Fit the spacer and 3rd gear pinion followed by ...

3.5c ... the thrust washer and circlip ...

3.5d ... then add the 4th gear pinion with the selector track inwards

3.5e Replace the thrust washer and then ...

3.5f ... replace the needle roller bearings, holding them in position with grease

3.5g Complete the reassembly of the roller bearings then ...

3.5h ... replace the 1st gear pinion over the bearings and add the thrust washer, followed by ...

3.5i ... the circlip ...

3.5j ... and the main bearing

3.5k Add 5th gear pinion to the other end of the layshaft, selector track inwards

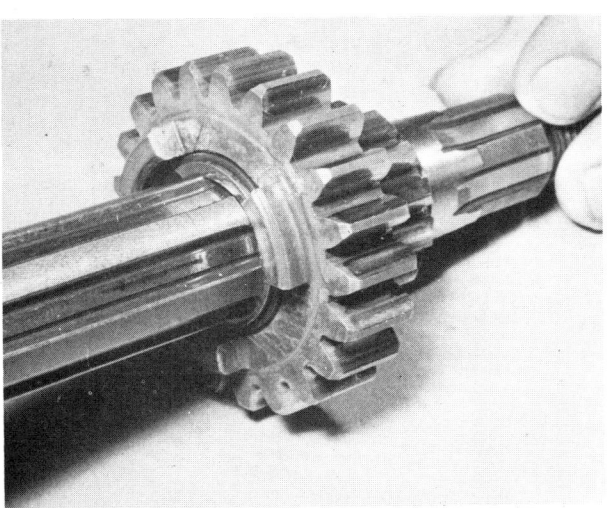

3.5l Retain 4th gear pinion with thrust washer and circlip. Bottom gear is integral with shaft

3.5m Next add the combined 3rd and 2nd gear pinion

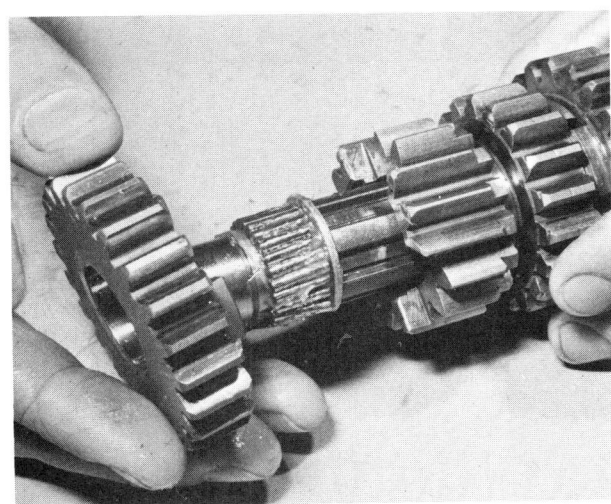

3.5n Followed by the thrust washer and needle roller bearings, then the 5th gear pinion

3.5o Add the thrust washer and circlip to complete the mainshaft assembly

Chapter 7: The TS250/1 model

3.5p Assemble both shafts with the selector forks located correctly

3.5q The selector drum can then be refitted ...

3.5r ... and the complete assembly inserted into the casing

3.5s The gearchange pawl and arm ...

3.5t ... in position

4 Kickstart

1 Reference to the accompanying illustrations will show the minor design changes that have occurred in the design of the kickstart mechanism. These do not affect either the dismantling or reassembly procedures given in the earlier section of this manual to any marked degree.

5 Front forks

1 The TS250/1 model has telescopic damped front forks that differ in construction from those used for the original TS250 model. It is therefore necessary to modify the working procedure when dealing with them.
Damage to the forks is likely to have occurred due to accident, rust, or general wear. If the machine has been involved in any type of accident the forks should be checked to see if they have been bent or twisted in any way. If the stanchions are slightly bent, it is possible to have them straightened by a dealer, otherwise the stanchion and possibly the whole leg may have to be replaced.

Chapter 7: The TS250/1 model

2 Rust may occur on the upper part of the stanchion, although this is not common in this particular case because of the well-designed gaiters provided. If the protective gaiter has been punctured or damaged rust will cause pitting of the stanchion and this will give rise to rough spots which will quickly wear out the fork seals. Worn seals are easily spotted for once they have started to fail, oil will be noticed leaking from them.

3 General wear of the fork legs can be easily assessed using the following method. Place the machine on its centre stand and tie down its rear end so that the front wheel is lifted well off the ground. Alternatively, ask a friend to sit on the pillion seat whilst the machine is on its centre stand; this will then raise the front wheel adequately. Take hold of the lower fork legs and try to move them backwards and forwards. Then try them from side to side. If any play is perceptible (and the head bearings are known to be in good order and are properly adjusted) the fork legs are worn and require attention.

4.1a Kickstart mechanism ...

4.1b ... in position

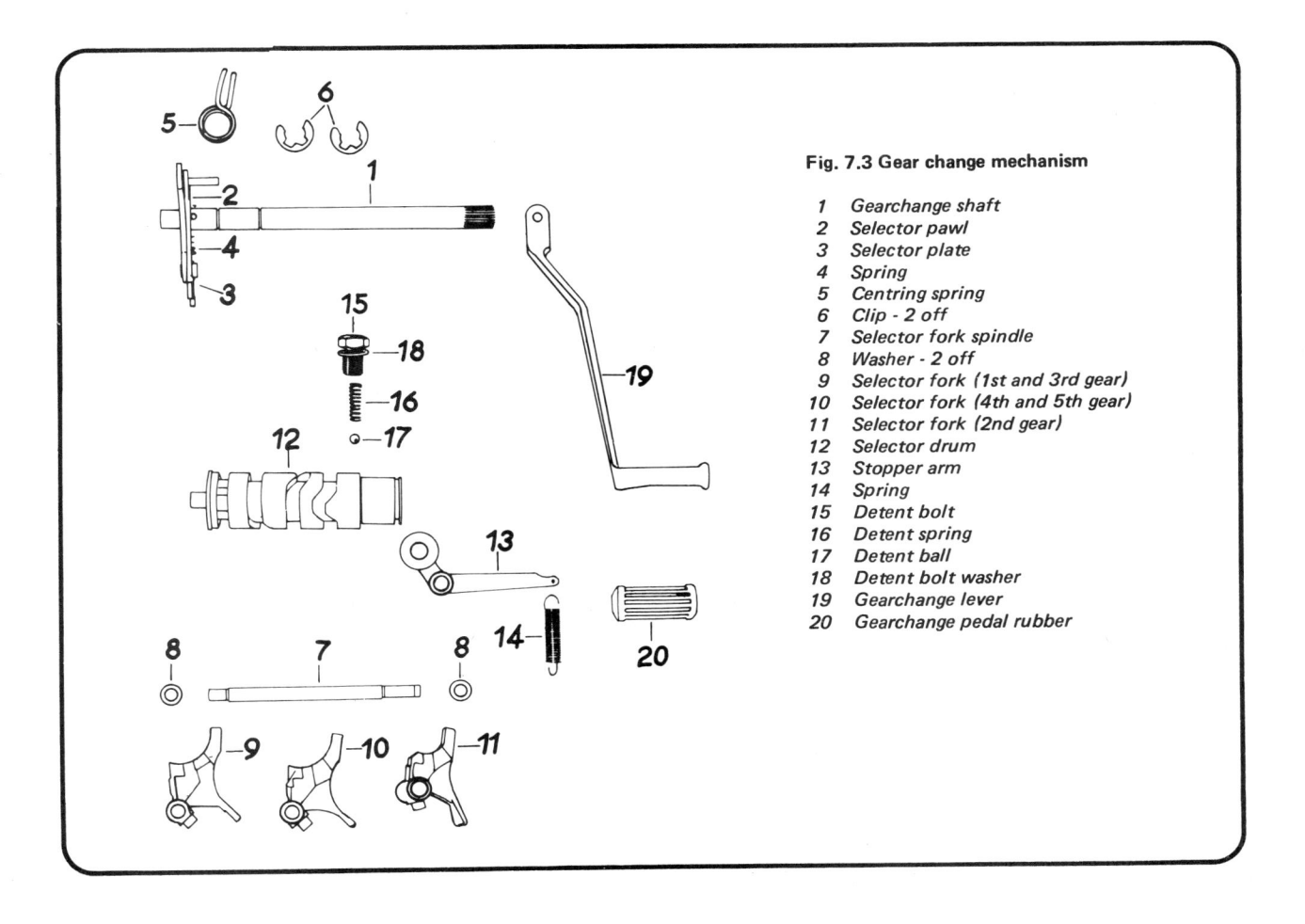

Fig. 7.3 Gear change mechanism

1 Gearchange shaft
2 Selector pawl
3 Selector plate
4 Spring
5 Centring spring
6 Clip - 2 off
7 Selector fork spindle
8 Washer - 2 off
9 Selector fork (1st and 3rd gear)
10 Selector fork (4th and 5th gear)
11 Selector fork (2nd gear)
12 Selector drum
13 Stopper arm
14 Spring
15 Detent bolt
16 Detent spring
17 Detent ball
18 Detent bolt washer
19 Gearchange lever
20 Gearchange pedal rubber

Chapter 7: The TS250/1 model

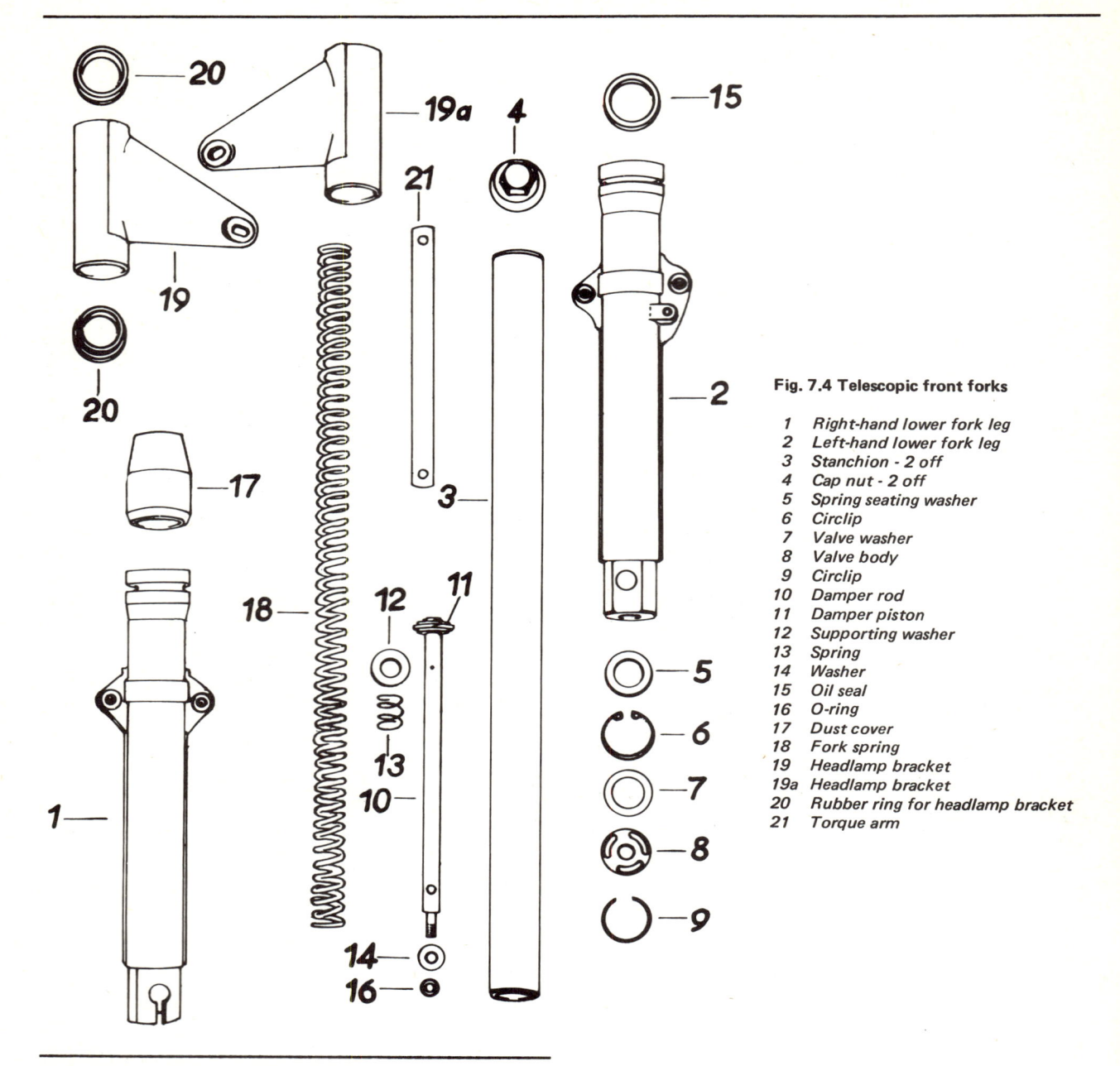

Fig. 7.4 Telescopic front forks

1. Right-hand lower fork leg
2. Left-hand lower fork leg
3. Stanchion - 2 off
4. Cap nut - 2 off
5. Spring seating washer
6. Circlip
7. Valve washer
8. Valve body
9. Circlip
10. Damper rod
11. Damper piston
12. Supporting washer
13. Spring
14. Washer
15. Oil seal
16. O-ring
17. Dust cover
18. Fork spring
19. Headlamp bracket
19a. Headlamp bracket
20. Rubber ring for headlamp bracket
21. Torque arm

6 Dismantling, renovating, and reassembling the fork legs

1 Assuming that the fork legs have been checked and it is necessary to dismantle them, the following procedure should be followed. Place the machine on its centre stand and tie down the back end. Alternatively, lay the machine on its side carefully (in this case it is probably best to remove the petrol tank first — see Chapter 2 section 2).

2 Remove both front wheel and mudguard (refer to Chapter 5 section 3).

3 Unscrew the top bolt, the clamp above the gaiter, and the gaiter clip. The whole fork leg may then be removed by gently pulling it downwards. Keeping the fork leg upright (to avoid spilling any of the fork oil which may be trapped in the top half of the stanchion) remove the fork spring by pulling it with your fingers. It should come out easily. Then turn the whole leg upside down and pump the lower leg and stanchion up and down whilst keeping the upper end of the stanchion over a container large enough to take the fork oil. When the fork leg is empty of oil dismantling may be continued. It is advisable to dismantle one fork leg at a time, to avoid the accidental interchange of parts.

4 Pull off the gaiter carefully.

5 To separate the stanchion from the lower fork leg it is necessary to remove the nut at the lower end of the fork leg. To remove this nut requires the use of a socket or sparking plug spanner of suitable size.

6 Withdraw the stanchion from the lower fork leg. The damper rod will be withdrawn at the same time. To separate the damper rod from the upper stanchion remove the oil seal, washer, spring and large washer from the end of the stanchion by inverting it carefully. Note: if the above mentioned components are not on the end of the damper rod when it is removed, they will still be inside the lower fork leg. It may be necessary to lever the tiny oil seal gently out of its seating using a piece of wire or something similar.

7 When the damper rod and its set of washers, spring and oil seal have been accounted for, place them to one side. It is useful to lay them out in the order in which they were removed, on a piece of paper.

8 Remove the circlip from the mouth of the stanchion, keeping a finger over the end as these components tend to fly out when the circlip is removed. Next remove the valve, valve washer, and spring. Beneath the spring is another circlip which retains the spring seating washer. Remove the circlip and take out the washer.

9 When the complete fork leg is dismantled and laid out, check each individual component for obvious signs of wear (eg. scratches or nicks). Check the piston ring on the damper rod as well for signs of wear. Replace any worn or damaged items and renew all oil seals as they are not very expensive and although they may not appear damaged or worn, it may save a lot of time and trouble to renew them whilst the leg is apart.

10 To reassemble the fork leg, reverse the dismantling procedure. Do not forget to replace the oil content (230 cc each leg).

6.3a Remove the fork leg cap bolt, then ...

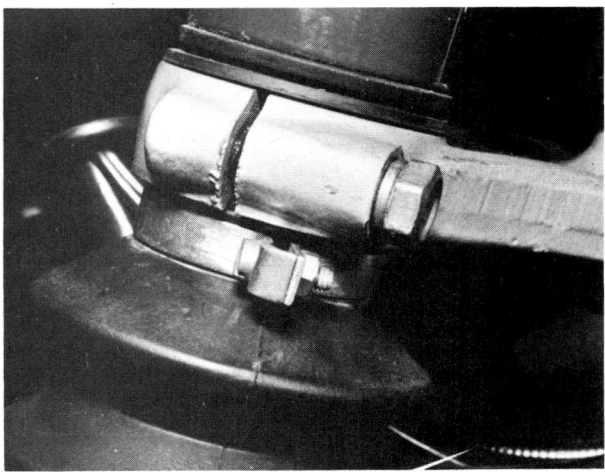

6.3b ... the bolt and gaiter clip

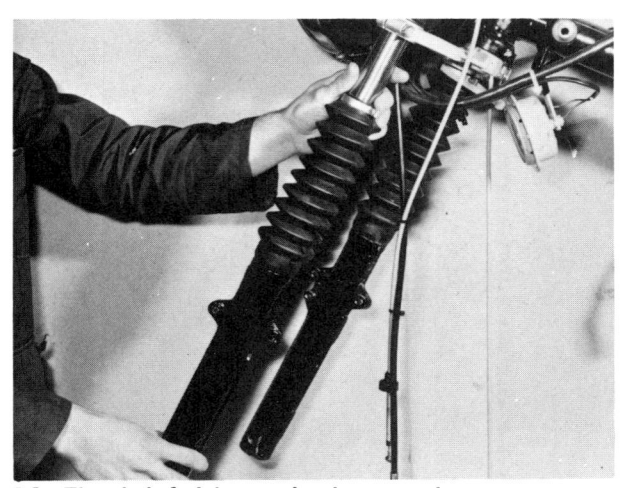

6.3c The whole fork leg can then be removed

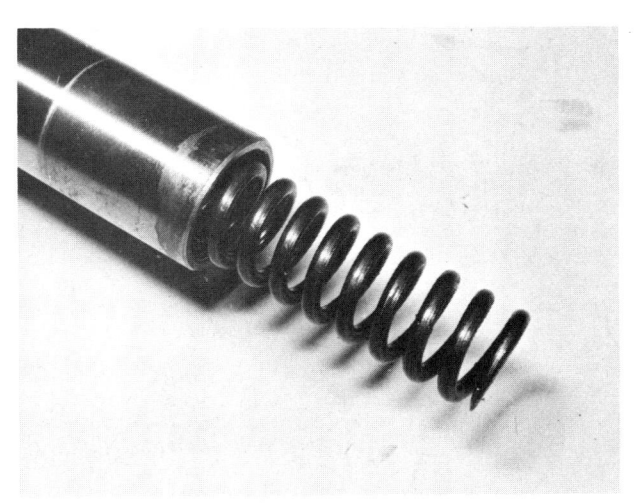

6.3d The spring can be lifted out

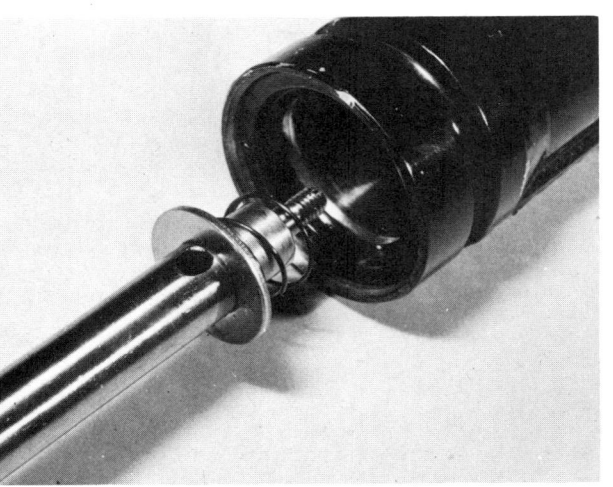

6.6 Withdraw the stanchion from the lower fork leg

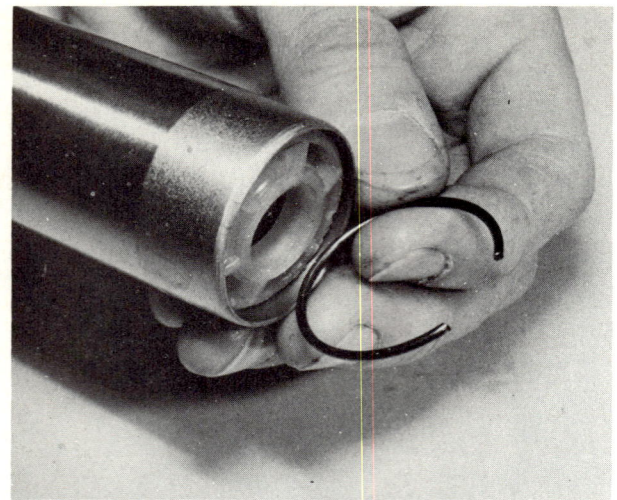

6.8a Remove the circlip and valve, followed by ...

6.8b ...the valve washer, and spring and ...

6.8c ... the circlip and spring seating washer

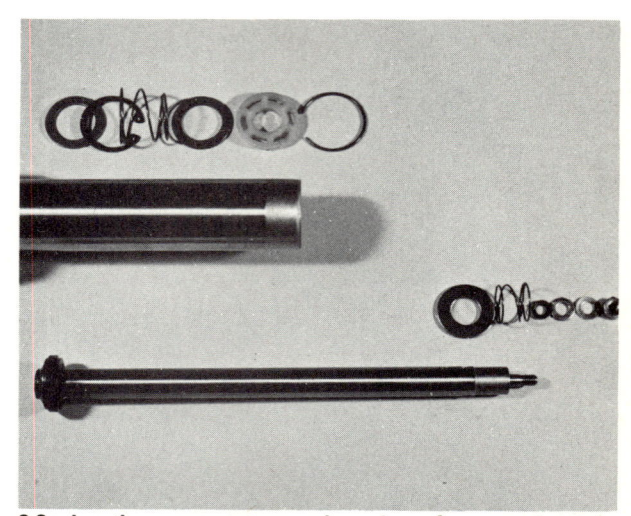

6.9a Lay the components on a clean piece of paper and examine for obvious signs of wear

6.9b Examine the piston ring and damper rod for wear

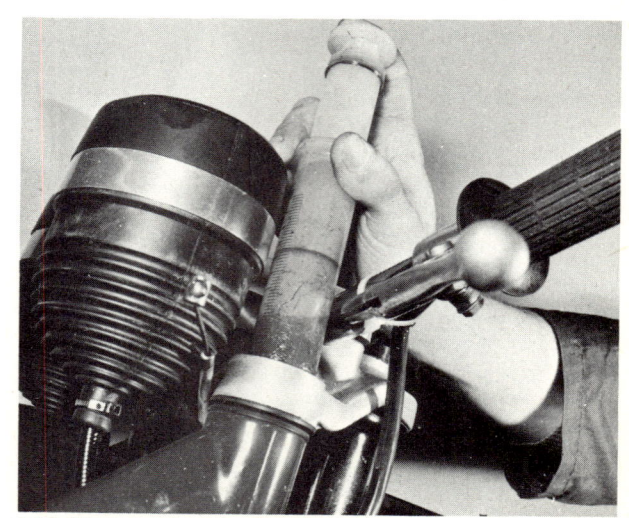

6.10 Replacing the damping oil with a syringe

Chapter 7: The TS250/1 model

7 Removal and replacement of the headlamp bulb

1 The accompanying photographs show the revised procedure for the removal and replacement of the headlamp bulbs.
2 It is first necessary to remove the headlamp unit from its casing. This is easily accomplished by undoing the two retaining screws.
3 Remove the unit, being careful to support it with the palm of one hand and turn it until it is at approximately 90° to the casing. This will expose the connectors as shown in 7.3. Pull off these connectors. The unit can then be removed completely from the machine.
4 Remove the retaining spring plate and parking light bulb (7.4).
5 The twin filament headlamp bulb can then be removed as shown in 7.5.
6 To reassemble, reverse the dismantling procedure.

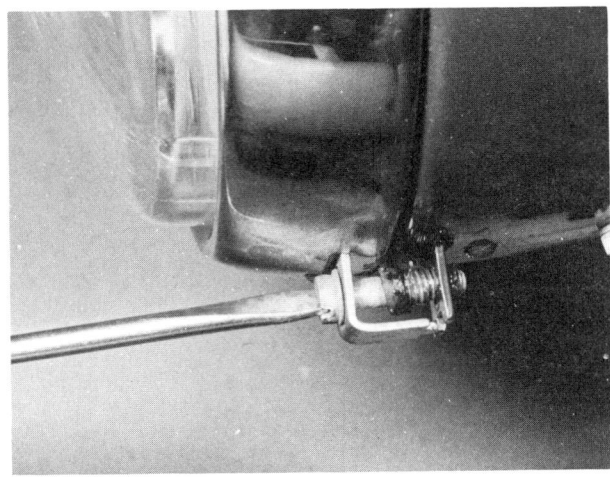

7.2 Unscrew the retaining screws

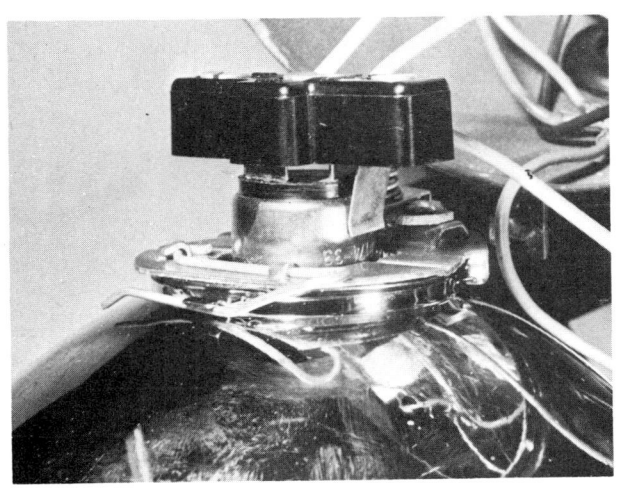

7.3 Remove the connectors

7.4 Remove the retaining spring and parking lamp bulb

7.5 The twin filament lamp bulb may then be removed

8 Removal and replacement of the tail/stop lamp bulbs

1 Remove the outer lens cover by unscrewing the two retaining screws. Be careful not to lose the rubber washers as these prevent accidental over-tightening of the retaining screws and also help to prevent water finding its way inside. When this casing has been removed, the lamp bulbs are easily taken out. (see 8.1). They have a bayonet fitting.

9 Removal and replacement of the flashing indicator bulbs

1 The removal of the flashing indicator lamp bulbs is very simple. Remove the outer lens cover by unscrewing the two retaining screws and the lamp bulb is easily accessible. It is of the bayonet fitting variety.

8.1 Remove the lens to reveal the lamp bulbs

9.1 Remove the lens for access to the lamp bulb

Wiring diagram key and colour code

(1) Headlamp
(a) Parking light
(b) Full headlight beam
(c) Passing beam
(d) Ignition-light switch
(e) Flasher unit
(g) Speedometer lighting
(h) Charging control light and flasher control light
(j) Idling indicating light
(k) Contact-tube strip, 2-pole
(2) Flashing light switch
(3) Combined dimmer switch
(a) Horn push-button

(b) Dimmer switch
(c) Push-button for by-pass light signal
(4) Horn
(5) Dynamo
(a) Contact breaker
(6) Ignition coil
(7) Sparking-plug
(8) Battery
(9) Idling switch
(10) Fuse box
(11) Regulator cutout
(12) Line connector

(13) Combined lighting fitting for stop, tail and number plate lights
(a) Stop light fitting
(b) Tail and number plate lighting fitting
(14) Stop light switch
(15) Flasher, front, left-hand side
(16) Flasher, front, right-hand side
(17) Flasher, rear, left-hand side
(18) Flasher, rear, right-hand side

Colour code:

sw = black   br = brown
ws = white   gr = grey
gn = green   bl = blue
rt = red   ge = yellow

Fig. 7.5 Wiring diagram for TS250/1 model

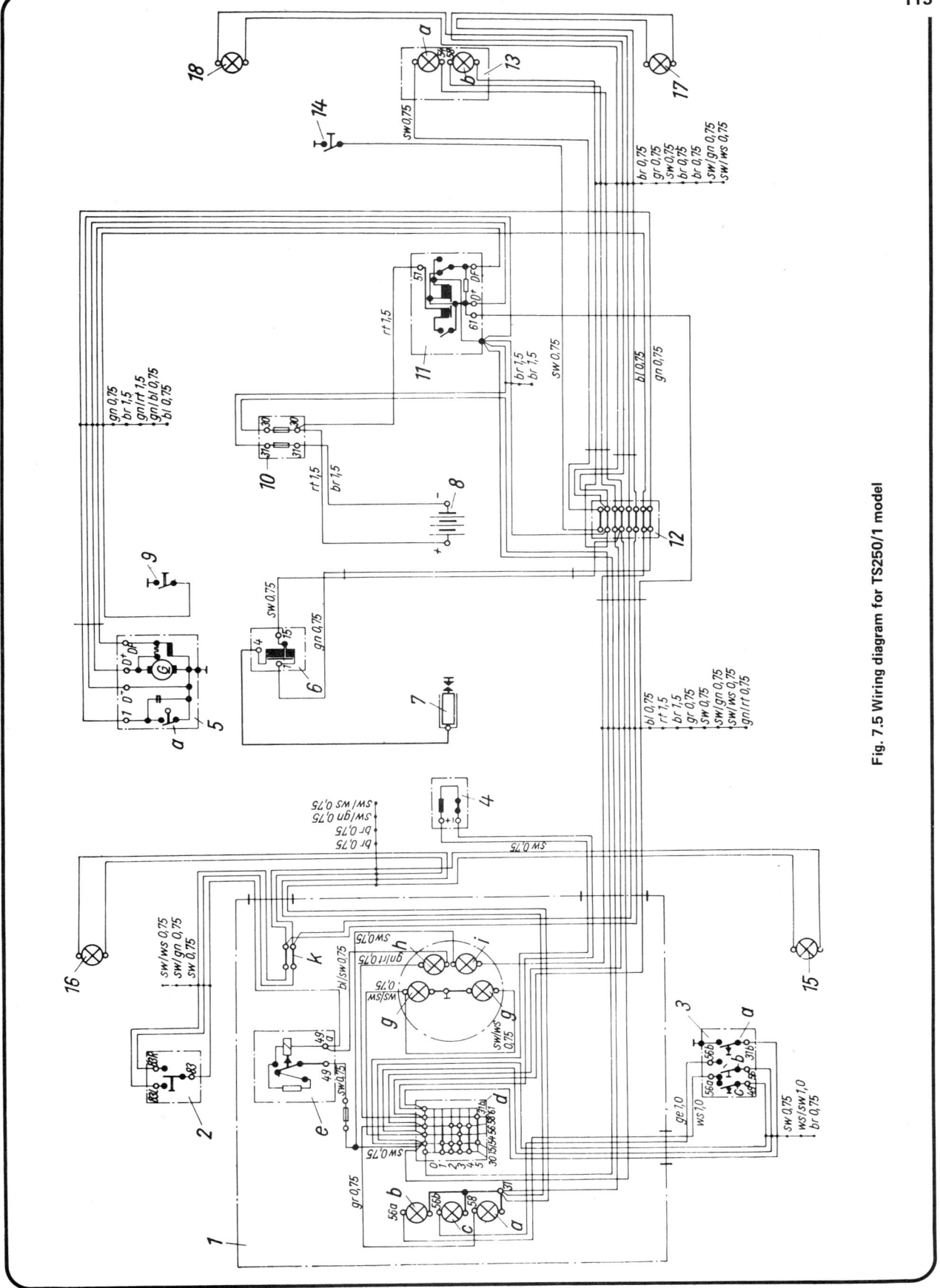

Metric conversion tables

Inches	Decimals	Millimetres	Millimetres to Inches		Inches to Millimetres	
			mm	Inches	Inches	mm
1/64	0.015625	0.3969	0.01	0.00039	0.001	0.0254
1/32	0.03125	0.7937	0.02	0.00079	0.002	0.0508
3/64	0.046875	1.1906	0.03	0.00118	0.003	0.0762
1/16	0.0625	1.5875	0.04	0.00157	0.004	0.1016
5/64	0.078125	1.9844	0.05	0.00197	0.005	0.1270
3/32	0.09375	2.3812	0.06	0.00236	0.006	0.1524
7/64	0.109375	2.7781	0.07	0.00276	0.007	0.1778
1/8	0.125	3.1750	0.08	0.00315	0.008	0.2032
9/64	0.140625	3.5719	0.09	0.00354	0.009	0.2286
5/32	0.15625	3.9687	0.1	0.00394	0.01	0.254
11/64	0.171875	4.3656	0.2	0.00787	0.02	0.508
3/16	0.1875	4.7625	0.3	0.01181	0.03	0.762
13/64	0.203125	5.1594	0.4	0.01575	0.04	1.016
7/32	0.21875	5.5562	0.5	0.01969	0.05	1.270
15/64	0.234375	5.9531	0.6	0.02362	0.06	1.524
1/4	0.25	6.3500	0.7	0.02756	0.07	1.778
17/64	0.265625	6.7469	0.8	0.03150	0.08	2.032
9/32	0.28125	7.1437	0.9	0.03543	0.09	2.286
19/64	0.296875	7.5406	1	0.03937	0.1	2.54
5/16	0.3125	7.9375	2	0.07874	0.2	5.08
21/64	0.328125	8.3344	3	0.11811	0.3	7.62
11/32	0.34375	8.7312	4	0.15748	0.4	10.16
23/64	0.359375	9.1281	5	0.19685	0.5	12.70
3/8	0.375	9.5250	6	0.23622	0.6	15.24
25/64	0.390625	9.9219	7	0.27559	0.7	17.78
13/32	0.40625	10.3187	8	0.31496	0.8	20.32
27/64	0.421875	10.7156	9	0.35433	0.9	22.86
7/16	0.4375	11.1125	10	0.39370	1	25.4
29/64	0.453125	11.5094	11	0.43307	2	50.8
15/32	0.46875	11.9062	12	0.47244	3	76.2
31/64	0.48375	12.3031	13	0.51181	4	101.6
1/2	0.5	12.7000	14	0.55118	5	127.0
33/64	0.515625	13.0969	15	0.59055	6	152.4
17/32	0.53125	13.4937	16	0.62992	7	177.8
35/64	0.546875	13.8906	17	0.66929	8	203.2
9/16	0.5625	14.2875	18	0.70866	9	228.6
37/64	0.578125	14.6844	19	0.74803	10	254.0
19/32	0.59375	15.0812	20	0.78740	11	279.4
39/64	0.609375	15.4781	21	0.82677	12	304.8
5/8	0.625	15.8750	22	0.86614	13	330.2
41/64	0.640625	16.2719	23	0.90551	14	355.6
21/32	0.65625	16.6687	24	0.94488	15	381.0
43/64	0.671875	17.0656	25	0.98425	16	406.4
11/16	0.6875	17.4625	26	1.02362	17	431.8
45/64	0.703125	17.8594	27	1.06299	18	457.2
23/32	0.71875	18.2562	28.	1.10236	19	482.6
47/64	0.734375	18.6531	29	1.14173	20	508.0
3/4	0.75	19.0500	30	1.18110	21	533.4
49/64	0.765625	19.4469	31	1.22047	22	558.8
25/32	0.78125	19.8437	32	1.25984	23	584.2
51/64	0.796875	20.2406	33	1.29921	24	609.6
13/16	0.8125	20.6375	34	1.33858	25	635.0
53/64	0.828125	21.0344	35	1.37795	26	660.4
27/32	0.84375	21.4312	36	1.41732	27	685.8
55/64	0.859375	21.8281	37	1.4567	28	711.2
7/8	0.875	22.2250	38	1.4961	29	736.6
57/64	0.890625	22.6219	39	1.5354	30	762.0
29/32	0.90625	23.0187	40	1.5748	31	787.4
59/64	0.921875	23.4156	41	1.6142	32	812.8
15/16	0.9375	23.8125	42	1.6535	33	838.2
61/64	0.953125	24.2094	43	1.6929	34	863.6
31/32	0.96875	24.6062	44	1.7323	35	889.0
63/64	0.984375	25.0031	45	1.7717	36	914.4

Metric conversion tables

1 Imperial gallon = 8 Imp pints = 1.20 US gallons = 277.42 cu in = 4.54 litres

1 US gallon = 4 US quarts = 0.83 Imp gallon = 231 cu in = 3.78 litres

1 Litre = 0.21 Imp gallon = 0.26 US gallon = 61.02 cu in = 1000 cc

Miles to Kilometres		Kilometres to Miles	
1	1.61	1	0.62
2	3.22	2	1.24
3	4.83	3	1.86
4	6.44	4	2.49
5	8.05	5	3.11
6	9.66	6	3.73
7	11.27	7	4.35
8	12.88	8	4.97
9	14.48	9	5.59
10	16.09	10	6.21
20	32.19	20	12.43
30	48.28	30	18.64
40	64.37	40	24.85
50	80.47	50	31.07
60	96.56	60	37.28
70	112.65	70	43.50
80	128.75	80	49.71
90	144.84	90	55.92
100	160.93	100	62.14

lbf ft to kgf m		kgf m to lbf ft		lbf/in^2 to kgf/cm^2		kgf/cm^2 to lbf/in^2	
1	0.138	1	7.233	1	0.07	1	14.22
2	0.276	2	14.466	2	0.14	2	28.50
3	0.414	3	21.699	3	0.21	3	42.67
4	0.553	4	28.932	4	0.28	4	56.89
5	0.691	5	36.165	5	0.35	5	71.12
6	0.829	6	43.398	6	0.42	6	85.34
7	0.967	7	50.631	7	0.49	7	99.56
8	1.106	8	57.864	8	0.56	8	113.79
9	1.244	9	65.097	9	0.63	9	128.00
10	1.382	10	72.330	10	0.70	10	142.23
20	2.765	20	144.660	20	1.41	20	284.47
30	4.147	30	216.990	30	2.11	30	426.70

Index

A

Air cleaner - 58
Automatic advance - 61

B

Barrels - cylinder - 18
Battery - 91
Brake: front - 78
    adjustment - 81
Brake: rear - 79
    adjustment - 81
    examination and renovation - 79
Bulb removal - 89, 113

C

Capacities - lubricants - 8
Carburettors:
    dismantling - 56
    float level - 60
    removal - 54
    settings - 56
Centre stand - 43
Charging light - 91
Cleaning - exhaust - 59
Clutch:
    examination and renovation - 19
    replacement - 24
Coil - ignition - 61
Condenser - 61
Contact breaker adjustment - 62
Crankcase - 19
Crankshaft - 18
Cush drive - 81
Cylinder barrels - 18
Cylinder head - 18

D

Dimensions and weights - 5, 101
Dynamo - 92

E

Earles type front forks - 70
Engine:
    dismantling - 12
    lubrication - 59
    mountings - 39
    reassembly - 19
    refitting in frame - 28
    running-in - 29
Exhaust - cleaning - 59

F

Fault diagnosis:
    brakes - 87
    carburettor and fuel system - 60
    clutch - 30
    electrical system - 93
    engine - 30
    frame and forks - 75
    gearbox - 30
    ignition system - 65
    lubrication system - 60
    tyres and wheels - 86
Filter - air - 58
Final drive - chain - 84
Footrests - 73
Forks - front:
    dismantling - 66, 110
    examination - 70
    removal - 66, 110
    replacement in frame - 70
Frame - examination - 73
Fuel tank - 53
Fuel tap - 53
Fuse location - 59

G

Gearbox:
    components - 17
    dismantling - 12
    examination and renovation - 19
    five speed TS250/1 - 103
    gear selector mechanism - 20
    lubrication - 59
    reassembly - 19

H

Headlamp - 89
Horn - 89

I

Ignition: coil - 61
    light switch - 88
    timing - 65

K

Kickstart - 15-35, 108

L

Lamps:
    direction - 89
    head - 89
    rear - 89
    stop - 89
Lubrication capacities - 8
Lubrication:
    engine - 59
    gearbox - 59

Index

M
Main bearings - 19
Maintenance - routine - 7
Metric conversion tables - 116, 117

O
Oil seals - 19
Ordering spare parts - 6

P
Petrol tank and tap - 53
Piston and rings - 18
Points - contact - 62
Primary chain - 19
Prop stand - 73

Q
Quick glance maintenance data - 8, 101

R
Recommended lubricants - 8
Regulator - voltage - 91
Rings - piston - 18
Routine maintenance - 7
'Running-in' - 29

S
Selector mechanism - 20
Silencer - 59
Spark plugs - 65

Specifications:
    clutch - 10
    electrical system - 8
    engine - 10
    frame and forks - 66
    fuel system and lubrication - 53
    gearbox - 10
    ignition system - 61
    wheels, brakes and tyres - 76
Speedometer and cable - 73
Sprocket - rear wheel - 84
Starting - rebuilt engine - 29
Steering head bearings - 71
Suspension units - 72
Stop lamp switch - 81
Swinging arm - 72

T
Technical specification - **See specifications**
Timing - ignition - 65
Tyres:
    removal and replacement - 85
    pressure - 76, 102

V
Voltage regulator - 91

W
Weights and dimensions - 5, 101
Wheels - 77
Wheel bearings - 77
Wiring diagrams - 95, 96, 97, 98-99, 115

Printed by
Haynes Publishing Group
Sparkford Yeovil Somerset
England